Grasping At The Wind

How to go from Ashes to Beauty Using God's Word-Practical Biblical Solutions For Complex Life Problems

Alfred T. Long Sr.

Copyright © 2008 by Alfred T. Long Sr.

Grasping At The Wind
How to go from Ashes to Beauty Using God's Word-Practical Biblical Solutions For Complex Life Problems
by Alfred T. Long Sr.

Printed in the United States of America

ISBN 978-1-60477-983-7

All rights reserved solely by the author. The author guarantees all contents are original and do not infringe upon the legal rights of any other person or work. No part of this book may be reproduced in any form without the permission of the author. The views expressed in this book are not necessarily those of the publisher.

Unless otherwise indicated, Bible quotations are taken from The Holy Bible, New Living Translation of the Bible. Copyright © 1998 by Stephen Arterburn and David Stoop.

www.xulonpress.com

Foreword

As a pastor, I reflect often on assignments given by God. If we look at some of the biblical greats, we find that their assignments caused them to travel on stormy paths. We find that their obedience or their disobedience sometimes produced great afflictions. God has what we call a furnace, an enclosed structure that manufactures grueling heat.

So goes the life of God's Generals. This book displays Alfred Long's life story in a brilliant narrative of incidents and experiences that caused him to capsulate the dialogue of a man bound by addictions. This awesome account of delivery and letting go unravels his total surrender to the Almighty God as he "Grasps at the Wind."

I watched as his life spiraled out of control and hope failed. I listened, as his rationalized wrong became right and right exchanged to wrong. I laughed with him on many occasions. I cried silently beside him watching him pick up the pieces of his shattered dream and begin to march and dance to the rhythm of a different beat.

In his book, "Grasping at the Wind", Alfred's' writing speaks volume to the life he lived. He often used prose and poetry to explain the challenge called life. *"The wind bloweth where it listeth and thou hearest the sound thereof, but canst not tell whence it cometh and whither it goeth John*

3:8 KJV). It was truly a call from God for him to put pen to paper to tell his story and share his life. His book takes you on a journey of building a true relationship with God using practical steps and biblical principles.

Having known Alfred Long for over thirty years, I consider myself one of his dearest friends. I saw first-hand the effects of these teachings on addiction and saw how it changed the lives of people struggling with dysfunctional behavior. Generational bondages broke as families sat in the classes together. Individuals who never faced their own addictions received deliverance. The transfer of addiction exposed the very works of Satan in the lives of believers. The methodology of recovery is simplified and easily grasped in this simple easy to read book.

This book is necessary have for pastors, lay people and sinners. Its principles are easy to grasp as Minister Long teaches us how to dissemble that bulletproof emotional shell to become productive citizens in the kingdom of God.

Pastor Bernice Garner – B.A.I.T. Ministry Christian Center, St. Louis Missouri

Table of Contents

Foreword v

Introduction xi

Prayer xv

Acknowledgements xvii

Poem – "Lord Please Help Me" xix

Part 1 – My Testimony 23

    Chapter 1 – The Beginning 25

    Chapter 2 - Watering the Seed of Rebellion 39

    Chapter 3 – Grasping at the Wind 47

    Chapter 4 - Babies and Fools 53

    Chapter 5 - Tricked, Bamboozled and Hoodwinked 57

Chapter 6 – Broken Clay 65

Chapter 7 – The Long Way Home 71

Part 2 - Working It Out 81

Chapter 1 – From Dysfunction To God's Function 83

1a – Discovery Questions 90

Chapter 2 – Overcoming Abuse 91

2a – Discovery Questions 96

Chapter 3 – Shame on You 97

3a - Discovery Questions 101

Chapter 4 – The Many Faces of Addiction 103

4a – Discovery Questions 107

Chapter 5 – Who is in Control? 109

5a – Discovery Questions 117

Chapter 6 –The Past Is Past 119

Part 3 – Biblical Applications For The Twelve Steps....123

    Chapter 1 – History of the 12 Steps...................125

    **Chapter 2 – Biblical Applications For The
                    Twelve Steps 131**

    Definitions 141

    Discovery Questions..143

    Poem – "Another Place"......................................145

    Conclusion 147

    Endnotes..149

Introduction

The objective of this book is twofold: I want to tell the wonderful things the Lord has done for me and to give some practical biblical solutions to those still suffering from addictions.

As we say in church, "You don't know like I know what God has done for me."

Similar to the demoniac in **(Mark 5: 1–20),** I lived among the tombs. I walked in the graveyard of alcoholism and drug addiction and instead of cutting myself with rocks, I ingested heroin into my veins. The laws of society could not restrain me as I plunged headlong towards death. God by his mercy and grace caught me before I destroyed myself. He saved, delivered and restored me to sanity. He gave me my life back.

Jesus commanded the former demoniac, *"No, go home to your friends, and tell them what wonderful things the Lord has done for you and how merciful he has been. So the man started off to visit the Ten Towns of the region and began to tell everyone about the great things Jesus had done for him; and everyone was amazed at what he told them Mark 5:19, 20 NLT).* Jesus gave this man a purpose for living and I believe He gave me the same purpose; to tell the world about the great things Jesus did for me!

In this book, I use my life story as a case study to analyze the different consequences of dysfunction and addiction and to give some practical biblical solutions for these problems. The first part of the book outlines my struggles with addiction, tracing my life from early childhood to adulthood. The second part of the book analyzes the consequences of a dysfunctional past. Moreover, how these consequences can affect our lives, even after we accept Jesus as our personal Savior. The book gives some biblical solutions to these consequences. The third part of the book applies Christian principles to a traditional twelve-step program.

This book is not just for alcoholics and drug addicts. The spiritual principles outlined in this book apply to everyone. If you substitute the word sin for addiction – which you can do – the net pulls us all in. Paul said in the Epistle of Romans, *"For all have sinned and fall short of God's glorious standard (Romans 3:23NLT)."* The Apostle John said, *"If we say we have no sin, we are only fooling ourselves and refusing to accept the truth (1John 1:8NLT).* This defines denial, the nemesis of recovery.

A robust recovery requires surrender to God's plan for our lives, which begins at Salvation. Dysfunction – which I define as not functioning as God intended - originated in the Garden of Eden with Adam and Eve. They enjoyed a perfect environment until they disobeyed God and sinned. That disobedience brought spiritual death, shame, blame and broken fellowship with God **(Genesis 3)**. The human race inherited sin and dysfunction from Adam. Paul said in Romans, *"When Adam sinned, sin entered the human race. Adams sin brought death, so death spread to everyone, for everyone sinned (Romans 5:12 NLT).*

Movie stars and television made addiction and recovery fashionable. The rich and famous regularly check themselves into luxurious resorts that double as recovery facilities. The paparazzi feed the publics insatiable appetite for gossip by recording their every move. HBO features a series called *Recovery* that capitalized on our fascination with addiction and the drama of recovery. Conversely, the real life consequences of substance abuse outweigh its entertainment value. Misery waits like a vulture, ready to claim the hapless victims that fall into the trap of addiction.

Jesus Christ is God's recovery program. Paul said, *"And what a difference between our sin and God's generous gift of forgiveness. For this one man, Adam, brought death to many through his sin. But this other man, Jesus Christ, brought forgiveness to many through God's bountiful gift. And the result of God's gracious gift is very different from the result of that one man's sin. For Adam's sin led to condemnation, but we have the free gift of being accepted by God, even though we are guilty of many sins. The sin of this one man, Adam, caused death to rule over us, but all who receive God's wonderful, gracious gift of righteousness will live in triumph over sin and death through this one man, Jesus Christ (Romans 5:15-17 NLT)* Recovery is renewed relationship with God. It removes the shame of sin and opens the door for access to God.

I do not advocate some magic, instant formula for recovery. As we cooperate with the Holy Spirit, he digs up the roots of our problems. Recovery requires some hard work and takes a lifetime. Nevertheless, God provides daily sustenance to nourish our minds and souls and strengthen us through the process.

My life still requires extensive work. I feel like Paul when he described himself as the chief of sinners **(1Timothy 1:15).** But like Paul said in the next verse, *"But that is why God had mercy on me, so that Christ Jesus could use me as a prime example of his great patience with even the worst sinners. Then others will realize that they too, can believe in him and have eternal life (1Timothy 1:16 NLT)."*

Alfred T. Long Sr.

Prayer

∞

Father, I pray for everyone myself included that reads this book. First, we praise and glorify you for who you are and for sending your Son Jesus to die for our sins. I ask that you help us become pliable and open to the move of your Holy Spirit. Search our hearts and expose anything that causes us to grieve you. Forgive us of the sin of selfishness and pride. Help us use the spiritual weapons we have at our disposal to tear down the strongholds of sin and addiction. Give us a hunger and thirst for your righteousness so our relationship with you is intimate and without guile. Help us to control our thought life by replacing our negativity with the promises of your Word. When the emotions of fear, doubt and disappointment flood our minds help us remember that you gave us power and authority over the enemy. Lord we thank you that we no longer have to live with shame because you abolished the condemnation in our life and nailed it on the cross of Jesus. I plead your blood over our lives because your blood covers our sins and gives us access into your presence. I thank you that we always have the victory and that your Holy Spirit makes intercession for us when we do not know what to pray for. Not only that but as our great High Priest, Jesus is at your right hand constantly praying for us. Lord, I give you all the praise, honor and glory and pray this and all prayers in the precious name of your Son Jesus Christ.

Acknowledgements

I acknowledge God first as head of my life and all people that continued to believe in me. To my children Lisa, Alfred Jr. and Tamar, I love you. To my granddaughter Tyler and granddaughter to be (yet unnamed), the cycle is broken. To my Pastor, Dr. Clark, who "lifts the lid" for my Shalom Church Family and me every time he preaches. To Bishop Crawford and congregation at the Israel Methodist Church in Chicago who had the courage to confront me and pray for me. To everyone who prayed for me because I know God answers prayer.

To Satin Booker who believed in me when everyone else left. I still have your note of encouragement.

I acknowledge my friends and staff at AT&T especially those that read this manuscript and gave me feedback without judging me.

I write this in loving memory of my family and friends who died before they could read this book: Bottie, my mother and father, my brother, my cousin Tony, Denise, and all my homeboys from the Nine who died before they lived

I give a special acknowledgement to the women at the Women's Eastern Reception Diagnostic and Correction Center in Vandalia, Missouri and the men at the Medium Security Institute in St. Louis City and those men and women incarcerated everywhere. Keep looking to God because if he changed my life he can and will change yours.

Space will not permit me to name everyone of influence in my life so if I missed anyone, charge it to my head not my heart.

"Lord Please Help Me"

Day breaks, and I got the shakes
My mind is numb and my body aches
I woke up this morning with those familiar heartaches
I drink some wine to maybe ease my mind
Hang on the corner to pass some time. I need some dope
That great false hope
Cause I cannot cope
I am about to let go of this rope.
Lord Please Help Me!

Yea, everybody plays the fool
Ain't no exception to that rule.
How did I get this way?
Well, let me see….
Is it my parents, my neighborhood, my teachers, my Blackness?
No, something is wrong with me.
I am angry, miserable, bitter and full of sin
Can anybody tell me when this will end?
When it started, I thought I was cool didn't follow any rules
School, that was for fools.
I played with life, like it was a toy

I thought I was a man but I was still a boy
I did not know the devil comes to steal, kill, and destroy
Game recognizes game or so they say
Players play, but you going to pay.
And when the reaper reaps
He is playing for keeps
Could be your life, now that's getting deep.
Lord Please Help Me!

Man, this corner is getting tight
I've been out here hustling all day and all night.
And it don't look like there's no relief in sight
Happiness I can't seem to find
And I'm about to lose my mind
Man, what happened to all the time?
Well! Well! Here come my lady, Ms Slim Shady
Hey sugar, help a brother please
You know you my main squeeze!
She laughed, Ha, Ha and said, "Fool you and me are through
I thought you knew."
But I didn't have a clue.
Let me go see my man, Pimping Joe.
Hey Joe, man hustling's been slow
And my money is low.
Brother, can I get a play, on a dime bag today?
So I can go somewhere and lay.
Joe said, "Man I ain't got time
To hear you whine
I've got to get mine!"
Lord Please Help Me!

Who is this walking down these bricks?
It's that sister from round the way; she used to turn
    tricks.
Heard she was saved, whatever that means
Now, a blind man can see that she's fresh and clean
I wonder if she got any green.
Hey yo, my sister, what did you say?
She looked through me and said, "Jesus is the Way!"
He died on the Cross-, for your sins to pay.
Confess with your mouth, the Lord Jesus
And that He rose, believe in your heart!
Jesus paid the price; can you do your part?
Pray with me, my brother, and, you will see
He'll unlock your soul and set you free!"
I said, "Girl, don't play with me
Can't you see, I'm in misery
All my life I've been praying,
Lord Please Help Me!"

Well I've tried everything else; I guess I'll try God
Maybe with the Lord on my side, life won't be as hard.
All I have to lose is this pain and shame
I can get out of this game
And obtain a new name.

Well, I asked Jesus in my heart and now I can say
I am a new creation; old things have passed away!
I finally have a Friend on whom I can depend
He said He would be with me until the very end!
God is real; He has given me hope.
I can cope and I do not need any dope!

If God did it for me, He will do it for you
Because every Word out of His mouth always comes true!
God answers prayer and now I can see
How He answered my prayer,
Lord Please Help Me!

Minister Alfred Long

Part 1

My Testimony

But the only letter of recommendation we need is you yourselves! Your lives are a letter written in our hearts, and everyone can read it and recognize our good work among you. Clearly, you are a letter from Christ prepared by us. It is written not with pen and ink, but with the Spirit of the living God. It is carved not on stone, but on human hearts (2Corinthians 3:2, 3 NLT).

Chapter 1

The Beginning

You watched me as I was being formed in utter seclusion, as I was woven together in my mother's womb. You saw me before I was born. Every day of my life was recorded in your book. Every moment was laid out before a single day had passed (Psalm 139: 15, 16 NLT).

Good morning, heartache here we go again
Good morning heartache
You're the one who knew me when
Might as well get used to you hanging around
Good morning heartache
Sit down. "Good Morning Heartache" – Billie Holliday 1956

A Day in the Life...

I awoke this morning with a pulsating, throbbing headache. It feels like a herd of elephants stampeding through my still groggy brain. I look at the alarm clock and it is noon. I look over at my cousin Tony, still asleep on the other twin bed in the bedroom we share at my parents' home. I say to me *"At least he took his clothes off."* I am still fully dressed with the clothes I wore yesterday. I was too high from drinking and shooting heroin the previous day to take them off before going to bed. I wake Tony and ask him how much money he has - because we need to buy some alcohol before we go to work at 3 p.m. I spent every dime I had - the night before - on alcohol and drugs. With trembling hands and shaky legs, I go to the kitchen for a drink of cold water. I can't eat solid food until I drink some alcohol to calm my nerves. I see myself in the hallway mirror and my condition shocks me. I weigh about 140 pounds on a six foot frame and look years older than my 20 years. Life in the fast lane makes you pay a toll. I look like *"a dying calf in a thunderstorm."* I'm twenty and hooked on drugs and alcohol. This day will turn out like all the rest – drinking and drugging until I am almost comatose. I'll stumble home and repeat the cycle the next day. A line from Marvin Gaye's' hit song, *"Inner City Blues"* runs through my mind, *"Oh, make you want to holler, the way they do my life, this ain't living, no, no baby this ain't living."* I needed some quick answers... before I stopped living.

I was born in Chicago, Illinois on July 14, 1952. My family and extended family lived at 204 E. 31st Street, at the intersection of 31st and Indiana, in the heart of the Bronzeville ghetto. I spent the first five years of my life here. We lived in a huge apartment building with a spacious backyard where all the children played.

My immediate family consisted of my father John, my mother Martha and my older brother John Jr. or Long John as they called him on the streets. We called him Buttons. My big brother was three years older than I was and could talk the skin off a leopard. I kept quiet at home because either my brother or father dominated every conversation.

My brother excelled as an athlete in grade school and won a scholarship, for basketball, to De La Salle High School.

Though small in stature, he possessed deft ball handling, passing skills and radar like shooting ability. A natural leader and point guard, he ran the basketball floor like his idol, the Hall of Fame point guard, Oscar Robertson.

De La Salle produced many leaders and had a strong academic program as well as athletics. The legendary Mayor Daley of Chicago graduated from De La Salle. De La Salle and other Catholic High Schools provided opportunities for many inner city athletes who otherwise might not have the money to pay for the education these schools provided.

My brother always decked himself out in the latest styles and ran with the in-crowd. Gregarious and outgoing, I thought he knew everyone in Chicago. His glibness endeared him to mostly everyone he met. We fought - like all siblings fight – mainly because I would sneak and wear his clothes. Lacking his flair for fashion, I usually destroyed his clothes while playing or just hanging out. This made him livid and we fought many rounds about his clothes.

Like so many other children of the ghetto, he had the potential to become whatever he desired but like the wicked servant in **(Matthew 25:14–30)** he buried his talents in the rocky soil of drugs and the street life. He squandered his scholarship and dropped out of high school in the tenth grade. He eventually became a heroin addict and shot drugs for over thirty years, was in, and out of prison most of his adult life and caused my parents much grief. This created a rift between us that God repaired later in our lives.

Coming from the same household, I guess we fought the same demons. Thankfully, in the last six or seven years of his life he finally kicked his drug habit. He fell in love, married, and worked a square job for the first time in his life. He conquered the beast of heroin addiction. In his last years, he used his speaking abilities to share his story at NA meetings around Chicago. I remember walking into a meeting while he spoke. My chest swelled with pride. He reminded me of the big brother I idolized as a child!

He died from cancer in 2006 however, by that time made his peace with God. His funeral resembled a homecoming of O.G's (original gangsters) from the "hood." They - and the Alderman of the Fifth Ward (where we grew up) - packed the church to pay their respects to a legend on the streets. He stayed true to the game and beat the odds. He died in peace with his wife Rochelle at his side. I preached his eulogy from **(Matthew 20:1-16).** He entered God's vineyard at the last hour but he ended with the same pay as everyone else.

I got before myself; let me go back to the beginning.

Thirty-First and Indiana represented one of the oldest African-American neighborhoods in Chicago. In its heyday, some of the finest Black nightclubs and eateries dotted 31st Street. Pimps, preachers, politicians, prostitutes and poor working class blacks combined to give thirty-First Street an air of excitement and vibrancy. Our apartment building dominated the northeast corner and straddled a half a block.

The surrounding neighborhood called Bronzeville birthed a plethora of African-American luminaries. Quincy Jones, Joe Louis and Lou Rawls come to mind, to name a few. Quincy Jones grew up a few blocks from my birthplace and he mentions in his book *"The Autobiography of Quincy Jones"* a character named Yellow.

He was a friend of Quincy Jones's father who worked as a carpenter for the numbers rackets. [1] I remember a character named Yellow who owned a paper stand that fronted for the numbers racket. I do not know if this was the same person mentioned in Quincy Jones' book but he sure fit the description. Yellow smoked a big, stinky cigar and loved to talk politics with my father. Yellow always gave us change to spend, so I did not mind the stinky cigar and the long wait for him and my father to conclude solving the world's problems.

Then, the numbers racket in Chicago thrived ran by Italian mobsters. During the first half of the twentieth century, the numbers racket provided jobs for many blacks excluded from the mainstream of society. Until the Italian Mafia took over, black gangsters ran the action. This underground economy pumped cash into the neighborhoods and kept many families from starving during the Depression era. It was an illegal lottery and almost everyone in the African-American community played hoping to "hit" and soften the blow of poverty most black families felt. Unlike today's drug dealers, the black numbers kings gave back to the community. They bankrolled black owned businesses that because of segregation, stayed in the neighborhood. They provided jobs for neighborhood residents who patronized the black owned businesses.

Segregation had its benefits. It forced the African-American community to band together. Teachers, doctors, lawyers, pimps, prostitutes, numbers runners, preachers, dope fiends lived in the same neighborhood. This gave children positive as well as negative examples to model their lives after. More options provided opportunities for better choices.

Today our inner cities resemble war zones with most of the middle-class long gone to escape the memories of poverty. Sadly, few ever look back to mentor and help those left behind. This perpetuates the vicious cycle of teen-age pregnancy, crime, alcohol and drug addiction, sub standard schools and hopelessness. Integration weakened the fabric of African-American neighborhoods. Villages that once raised African-American Kings and Queens became ghettos that manufacture gang bangers and dope dealers. This keeps the prison industry and funeral homes booming with business.

Thirty-First and Indiana, by the time of my birth had started to lose her luster. Ravaged by time and neglect, the neighborhood faced destruction. Everyone saw the wrecking balls coming and wanted out including my family. Today the old neighborhood bustles with the excitement of gentrification. Builders turned run down, long deserted structures into condominiums that now sell for close to a million dollars. However, the Illinois Institute of Technology bought and replaced my old dwelling and turned the land into a parking lot.

Of course, as a child you cannot recognize or fully understand the implications of your upbringing. Some events however etched themselves in my memory. I remember the O.K. candy store located across the street from our apartment building. We bought candy and toys from that store. I bought my first hula-hoop there, when hula-hoops first came on the scene. Tootsie or one of the other "big" girls from my building escorted me across thirty-First Street to make my candy and toy purchases. With curly hair, and dreamy eyes the older girls doted on me. I look at old pictures of myself and wonder what happened. I guess age catches us all.

The children played in a huge backyard under the watchful eyes of the adults sitting on their back porches. One day, this little bully named Chucky singled me out for some verbal abuse. He picked on all the children because he came from a tough family. Everyone feared his older brother, Johnny B, who wore a process and ran with a gang. Chucky and I started fighting. I grabbed his eye and tried to snatch it out of the socket. The adults broke us up. My father beamed with pride when he heard about the fight. The positive reinforcement he gave me made me feel good. Chucky, Johnny B and I met up later in life; this time we drank wine and shot dope together. Chucky and Johnny B died long ago from drug and alcohol abuse.

Most of all I remember the fighting and drinking at home. The adults in my family loved to party and alcohol freely flowed. My father, an alcoholic, drank more than anyone did. Typically, the parties started innocently however, they ended in arguments and fights, with my father usually initiating the battles. He carried a lot of internal bitterness and alcohol intensified those feelings. He frequently unloaded that anger on my mother, verbally abusing her until he fell off to sleep, too drunk to continue his venomous tirades. His abuse of my mother made me hate him when he drank, yet love him when he sobered up, and then hate him again. These feelings perplexed me and prepared my heart for the seeds of rebellion that took root.

My father was born June 22, 1913 in Birmingham, Alabama. Birmingham became a city in 1871. Iron ore, coal and limestone abounded in the land in and around Birmingham. As a result, steel mills sprouted up providing jobs for blacks weary of sharecropping for little or no profit. During the turn of the century, Birmingham became the industrial capitol of the South. Birmingham oozed racism as blacks and whites competed for the steel mill jobs. During the Civil Rights Movement, Birmingham received the nickname "Bombingham" because of the frequent bombings at the hands of segregationists and racists. The bombing at the 16th Street Baptist Church, in September 1963, where four little girls died shocked the nation with its brutality and lack of concern for human life. This sad event exposed the festering, infected sore of racism and helped usher in the passage of the Civil Rights Bill, in 1964, signed by President Lyndon Johnson.

My grandfather had straight white hair and called my father darling. His mixture of Indian, Caucasian and African-American blood gave him an exotic look. He was born in 1894, in Elmore County, Alabama to my great-grandfather Gilbert, born in 1874, and my great-grandmother Josephine.

Gilbert's father and my great-great grandfather Abe was born in 1830 in Elmore County, Alabama. The 1880 census listed my great-great-grandfather as a mulatto, which meant his parents had a mixture of white and/or Indian blood combined with black blood. The 1880 and 1910 census listed both my great-grandmother Josephine and great-great grandmother Betsy as black.

Elmore County, located on the outskirts of Montgomery Alabama, straddled a region called the Black Belt. The soil in the Black Belt region proved exceptionally productive for growing cotton. This region extended from Texas to Virginia and produced many plantations in the antebellum South.

After the Thirteenth Amendment abolished slavery in 1865, many freed slaves remained on plantations working as sharecroppers. They barely eked out a living because of the unfair practices of ex-slave owners and Jim Crow laws designed to keep the African-American race in bondage despite the passing of this law. Usually ex-slaves took the last name of their ex-owners and worked the land of their old plantations. Through research, I found out that, two large plantation owners in Elmore County, during that time, had the last name of Long. My great-great grandfather Abe probably adopted that surname and passed it to us. My ancestors stayed close to the land. The Thirteenth Amendment freed their bodies but their minds remained imprisoned with a psychological slavery passed down to generations of African-Americans who still struggle to throw off the remnants of the horrific conditions of slavery.

Elmore County did not provide much opportunity for blacks outside of sharecropping and remains one of the poorest sections of the country. My grandfather left the hardscrabble farm life in Elmore County to pursue an industrial job in Birmingham. The hot, dangerous steel millwork did not appeal to him so he became a barber. He married my grandmother Ellen who gave birth to my father in 1913. He named my father John, after himself. My father was the oldest of five children.

I remember, as a child, my family rode a train to Birmingham, to visit my grandfather. He lived by some railroad tracks that separated east and west Birmingham. My brother and I loved to play on those tracks. One day, some white kids from the other side of the tracks started throwing rocks at us. We retaliated by throwing rocks back at them. We did not understand the rules of racism. Suddenly, my grandfather rushed us into the house. My brother and I did not understand the fuss until the adults chided us for throwing rocks at white children. Birmingham seethed with bigotry during this time and our innocent childhood game could turn to death. This incident introduced me to the sinister, malevolent face of racism.

Emmitt Till, another lad from Chicago, allegedly flirted with a white woman in Money Mississippi, in 1955. For this violation, a mob mutilated, killed and threw him in the river. His mother showed pictures of his battered face to the world, choosing to give him an open casket funeral. That explained and I later understood why the adults feared for our lives. We did not leave the house until our family returned to Chicago.

My father left Birmingham during the Depression era. I heard though cannot substantiate stories that he killed a boy for stabbing his younger brother Zack to death. He arrived in Chicago during the Depression era with few opportunities for employment. He stayed with my grandmother Ellen who years earlier left my grandfather, remarried and moved to Chicago. They lived at thirty-eighth and Federal, an old black neighborhood later torn down to make room for the projects.

He found work as a parking lot attendant for downtown garages owned by the Italian Mafia. His boss, Ben Ponzio, was the son-in-law of Paul "The Waiter" Ricca. Paul "The Waiter" Ricca worked for Al Capone during Capone's reign as boss of the Chicago Mob. When Capone went to prison in 1932, for tax evasion, Paul "the Waiter" Ricca along with Frank Nitti took over as heads of the Chicago Mob. Frank

Nitti committed suicide leaving Mr. Ricca as sole head of the Chicago mob. Ricca went to prison in 1943 for extorting money from the movie industry in Hollywood. He served three years, before the government paroled him. After prison, he shunned the limelight, and kept a low profile. He became the elder statesman of the Chicago mob giving orders to his successors, Tony Accardo and Sam Giancama from the background. Ricca died in 1972 of natural causes. [2] He loved my father for his feistiness, intelligence and excellent work ethic.

My father fought at the least provocation. He weighed 165 pounds, at most, and stood about 5 feet 11 inches tall. However, he demanded respect from everyone. When mad, my father morphed into an Incredible Hulk type character that made him appear larger than his actual size. He intimidated men twice his size. Neighborhood bullies shied away from my brother and me because my father did not allow anyone to mess with his family. Instead of catcalls and whistles, the corner boys called my mother Mrs. Long or they paid a price. He kept a pistol and did not mind using it.

My father worked hard, even when he drank, and instilled that work ethic in me. He taught me the importance of performing your job with a spirit of excellence. Though a parking lot attendant, he took pride in his work and considered himself the best car hiker in Chicago. He often took me on jobs with him and I saw first-hand how hard he worked. He always taught me that any job worth performing was worth performing to the best of my ability.

My mother was born August 21, 1926 in Tuscumbia, Alabama in Colbert County. My grandmother, Inez Braden never talked about my mothers' father. From rumors, I heard he was a white man who abandoned my grandmother and mother. They called my mother a "barn baby." This derogatory term - that originated in the rural South - described babies born to interracial couples. These couples usually conceived these babies away from public scrutiny and the spotlight of racism. Usually, this occurred in a barn or some back room. Typically, the baby grew up in the African-American community because one drop of black blood deemed you black. The circumstances around my mother's birth remain a mystery to me.

My grandmother, Inez Braden, was born in Colbert County, Alabama in 1907 to Patty and Joe Braden. Patty and Joe worked as sharecroppers and lacked formal education like most farm workers from that era. Colbert County, Alabama lied in the foothills of the Appalachian Mountains in Northwest Alabama near the coast of Tennessee. My grandmother was the middle of five children and I called her Nana. The family called my grandmother Little Inez because her parents named her after Patty's twin sister, a woman we called Bottie.

My mother moved to Chicago in the 1930's along with my grandmother, aunts and cousins from Alabama. Her great-aunt Bottie raised her and made sure she went to private schools. She met my father as she worked behind the counter of a drugstore in Bronzeville. She was 16 at the time and stunningly beautiful. She had a light complexion with beautiful eyes. People say she resembled Lena Horne, considered one of the most beautiful women in the world. My father was 29 and love struck. He vowed to marry her when she grew up. Story has it; my father scared all of her young suitors away with his reputation as a fighter that carried a pistol. My grandmother resented my father because she hoped my mother would marry one of the nice, respectable boys in the neighborhood. I guess love overcame reason because they eventually wed in April 1949.

My mothers' great-aunt and my great-great aunt Bottie, real name, Inez McDale was the matriarch of our family. Bottie was born in Colbert County, Alabama in 1885.

Bottie came to Chicago during one of the first African-American migrations from the rural South to the Northern cities. These cities promised relief from the stifling racism and backbreaking farm work, in the South. She lacked formal education but abounded with common sense. Bottie ran a brothel during the Depression era and despite her lack of education, had a keen business mind. She could not perform calculus or algebra but she could count and save money. She resembled Mary Bethune McLeod, the great African-American educator, with the same formidable stature and demeanor.

My older cousins tell stories of some of the famous people that frequented Bottie's brothel, from Ralph Capone - brother of Al Capone - to Duke Ellington who liked to bring his band to Chicago. Rollicking, rambunctious and rowdy Chicago provided her with open doors to use her innate entrepreneurial skills. In another time or place, with the benefits of an education, she could have run her own corporation

Bottie helped everyone in the family because she kept money and had a gigantic heart. My father respected Bottie along with most people that met her. The nature of her business gave her a tolerance for human frailty. She saw society's elite during the day turn into perverted pursuers of forbidden flesh at night. Her non-judgmental attitude endeared her to many of society's outcasts. I think - more than anyone - she understood my father.

Bottie did not have children of her own. She took care of the children in the household while our parents worked. She considered me her favorite and went out of her way to spoil me. During the day, we watched her favorite baseball team, the Chicago Cubs play. I can still hear her rooting for Ernie Banks to hit a homerun. On Sunday evenings, we listened to the Reverend Clarence Cobbs, Pastor of the First Deliverance Church preach the gospel. A flamboyant preacher, Reverend Cobbs, befriended the gangsters and numbers kings of Bronzeville and had a large congregation. Bottie stopped physically attending church; but she did not miss a Sunday broadcast.

She babied me, allowing me to suck a bottle against my parents' wishes. I secretly nursed a bottle until I entered kindergarten, with Bottie's blessing, until I finally decided to give it up to avoid embarrassment. I loved that woman for giving me my way! Even then, you could see the seeds of rebellion and deception growing in my young personality.

Bottie died in 1962. Her death left a huge void in our family, especially in me. She wielded a huge influence over me and I missed her. We became latchkey children. This left us children with plenty of time for mischief. I took full advantage of those unsupervised hours, hanging out with my friends. Bold and mischievous, I gravitated towards other naughty children. I started an infatuation with the streets that later blossomed into a full-blown love affair.

Psychologists and behavioral therapists teach that 90% of your personality forms in the first five years of your life. Dr. Henry Cloud said in his book *"The Secret Things of God", that research has shown that it is possible to predict the later academic success of five year olds by measuring certain character traits over and above IQ. When they followed five year olds long term into high school and beyond, how smart they were did not predict success as well as their ability to delay gratification. The group that could delay gratification at age five outperformed kids who were smarter than they were, later on in high school was, but who lacked that character trait.* [3] I performed well on IQ tests, but lacked the ability to delay gratification. This character trait caused me many headaches and heartaches later in life.

Chapter 2

Watering The Seed Of Rebellion

"Only fools say in their hearts, "There is no God." They are corrupt and their actions are evil; no one does good (Psalm 14:1)!

*Mother, mother, mother
There's too many of you crying
Brother, brother, brother
There's far too many of you dying. "What's Going On" - Marvin Gaye 1972*

My infatuation with the streets paralleled my worsening behavior at school. I remember writing a note to my second grade teacher cursing her with the language I heard at home. When she read the note, her face went pale, then crimson, as I defiantly stared at her. Of course, they notified my parents, who lightly reprimanded me. In a childish way, I yearned for my fathers' approval and felt that if I cursed as he did, I would gain his approval.

Integration opened housing in Chicago in the late 1950's and our families moved to a neighborhood called Chatham. Chatham was a neighborhood of solid brick apartment buildings and homes with beautifully manicured lawns. Ernie

Banks, the Hall of Fame baseball player and Mahalia Jackson, the world-renowned gospel singer, lived in Chatham.

As children, we often knocked on Ernie Bank's door to solicit empty pop bottles to redeem for money. When he answered, to his credit, he graciously and patiently put up with our intrusion on his privacy. I remember his eyes, the kindness in them, as he gave us pop bottles. His stature as a star baseball player did not make him arrogant and aloof. On the other hand, we did not approach the home of Mahalia Jackson. It stood at the end of a long driveway and looked large and forbidden to us children. I settled for watching her on T.V and listening to her records.

Many African-American lawyers, doctors, politicians and plain old hard working blue-collar people lived in Chatham. Chatham represented a social climb for my family and my brother and I went to Catholic School with the children of these movers and shakers of the community. Deep inside, I felt that my home life did not measure up to theirs. I felt ashamed of my home life as I imagined the bliss these well off children enjoyed at home. I later found out, their home life mirrored mine in many ways; they just presented a prettier façade.

My family was one of the first African-American families to move into Chatham. White families moved out as black families poured into Chatham. We left thirty-First Street and did not look back. My parents enrolled my brother and me in St. Dorothy Catholic School where I received, despite my rebelliousness, an excellent education. From the outside our lives looked bright, new neighborhood, new schools, new friends but the inside problems persisted. My father's drinking became worse and he became more abusive towards my mother.

Academics came easy for me. I routinely topped my class without serious study or homework. I routinely copied my homework from the other smart children before classes began. Most days, I could not concentrate in school because my father cursed and argued all night. This broke my rest and I went to school tired and angry. I acted out for attention because negative attention beats no attention. This infuriated and saddened my teachers because they saw my potential and knew I needed some intervention before the streets sucked me into a web of destruction. Two of my teachers stand out, in my mind, even today because of their caring natures.

Mrs. Miller, my third grade teacher, took a special interest in me. She recognized my potential and in my young eyes, Mrs. Miller was the most beautiful woman in the world. I developed a schoolboy crush for her. She let me clean the blackboard and stay after school to help her finish projects. She talked to me and listened when I talked. She lived on my block so she knew about my background. She showed me love and I performed in her class, I even did homework. Catholic nuns taught most classes at St. Dorothy however, Mrs. Miller represented one of the few lay teachers at the school. At the end of the school year, I regretted leaving her class because I felt that she genuinely cared for me and I flourished in that environment.

Amid my rebelliousness, I remember some early spiritual stirrings. I built little altars in my room to pray and meditate. At one time, I even considered entering the priesthood. Of course, I did not share this with my friends for fear of ridicule. I felt this tug-of-war in my young heart between the streets and my spirituality. When I meditated in my room, I felt a serenity that shortly erased the anger, fear and loneliness that plagued me. I needed guidance from someone to help me nurture my spirituality. However, what you feed grows and I spent more time in the streets than I did meditating so eventually I stopped meditating altogether.

This continued until seventh grade when Sister Mary Ellen showed me some love. She also recognized my potential and attempted to rescue me from delinquency because by the seventh grade I had already made a pact with the streets. She allowed my friend Ernie Curd and I to stay at her parents farm in Jessup, Iowa. Jessup, population about six hundred, gave us city boys another view of life. We worked on the farm and experienced how a functional family operates. We ate dinner at the table in the evening and went to church on Sunday.

This experience also taught me the senselessness of racism and showed me that love is colorblind. I remember the shock on some of the parishioners faces the first Sunday Ernie and I walked into church. For some children, we represented the first black people they ever saw close up. Still, Sister Mary Ellen's family adopted us as one of the family. I cherish those memories but by that time, the streets had her claws in me.

My friends attended the public schools and lived in the rougher areas of Chatham. We played football and baseball in the alley because the owners the houses and apartment buildings wanted to preserve their front lawns. We shot marbles, fought, stole, and climbed roofs, played on the railroad tracks, teased the girls and did whatever children did in the early 1960's. Mischievous and rebellious, we stayed in trouble. Most of my friends came from the same background I came from. They came from two parent homes that outwardly looked successful however on the inside dysfunction prevailed. Our parents worked hard to maintain their lifestyle. This left little time for us. Children need spiritual and emotional nurturing, even more than a beautiful home and the latest fashions. This nurturing prepares children for life and safeguards them from booby-traps and land mines hid behind the false promises of happiness offered by the world.

Our dysfunction linked us in a slow dance with death and despite our nice neighborhood; the majority of us became drug addicts and/or alcoholics. We started forming gangs, engaging in petty crime and fistfights. We gathered at the blue light basement parties, community centers and danced to the Motown hits of the 1960's. Usually before the night ended, someone would start a fight to end the evening on a violent note.

Each gang claimed a street as their territory. The 71st street Bowery Boys, the 75th street Syndicate, the 79th street Ambassadors and Crystal Counts, the 83rd street Egyptian Lords and the 95th street Syndicate all staked their claim to real estate they did not really own. We pledged allegiance to street corners owned by the city. My friends and I started the 79th street Ambassadors. The gangs fought each other on the weekends and went to school together during the week. Rival gangs would pummel you with fist and feet, if they caught you in their territory. Every gang had their boxing champion who was especially good with his hands. The champions would bob and weave, imitating Muhammad Ali. Ali, the former Cassius Clay, paid frequent visits to 79th street because of the Muslim Mosque and many Muslim owned businesses located in the area. He playfully shadowboxed with us children as he screamed, "I'm the Greatest!" This was before he beat Sonny Liston in 1965. We loved him and went into mourning when he lost his first fight to Joe Frazier. We admired him because he stood up to the establishment and came out with his manhood intact. Our neighborhood produced some boxing virtuosos that knew how to "throw some hands." We did not need guns.

This changed in the mid to late 1960's with the growth of the Blackstone Rangers, led by Jeff Fort and the Gangster Disciples, led by Larry Hoover. These charismatic gang leaders took gangbanging to a new level. They had extraordinary organizational skills and ran their gangs like corporations. They pioneered the concept of the mega gang and helped birth the gang explosion throughout the nation.

The Bloods, Crips, and the mega gangs of today borrowed their tactics from these two gangs. Both Fort and Hoover reside at the super maximum-security facility in Florence, Colorado, serving life sentences. They chose a lifestyle of murder and crime when they both owned the organizational and leadership abilities to run any Fortune 500 Company in America. What a waste of talent and intelligence however, this sad saga repeats itself from generation to generation. Jails and prisons are loaded with super talented individuals that made wrong choices from limited options.

The proliferation of drugs and illegal profits from selling drugs sparked the killing and drive by shootings. Gangs fought over turf as gangbanging became big business. The Blackstone Rangers and Disciples started recruiting in our neighborhood, Chatham. Recruiting meant that you joined the gang or face serious physical harm, in some cases death. However, by that time my friends and I pursued drugs. The neighborhood gangs that fought on the weekends now shot dope and drank wine together. The mega gangs left us alone because our loyalty belonged to drugs instead of gangs. The harvest for potential gang bangers provided them enough members with out recruiting some addicts and we fattened their coffers with our drug purchases.

Gangs satisfied the same needs as drugs and alcohol. They provided a false sense of security. They built up your self worth and gave you a purpose for living. You aligned yourself with people that understood you to give you a sense of belonging and love. In addition, the illegal money made through various criminal activities provided opportunities to accumulate the material goods that represented the American Dream. True gang members will die for the gang, or end up in the penitentiary honoring some senseless code.

As my friends and I grew older, we developed a fatalistic nihilism that convinced us we would die before the age of 30. Mavis Staples' song from the 60's, "Respect Yourself", described us. She sang, *"If you think that the world owe you something cause you here, you're going out the world backwards like you did when you first came here, respect yourself."* We did not respect ourselves or anyone else for that matter and we reaped what we sowed.

I liken the streets to the adulterous woman in Proverbs. King Solomon said, *"Now then, my sons listen to me; pay attention to what I say. Do not let your heart turn to her ways or stray into her paths. Many are the victims she has brought down; her slain are a mighty throng. Her house is a highway to the grave, leading down to the chambers of death (Proverbs 2:18, 19 NLT)."*

Chapter 3

Grasping at the Wind
⧖

So again it is all meaningless like grasping at the wind (Ecclesiastes 2:26b, 4:16b NLT

And I ain't seen nothing but trouble baby
Nobody really understands, no no
And I go to the place where the good feeling awaits me
Self-destruction in my hand
Oh Lord, so stupid minded
Oh and I go crazy when I can't find it
Well I know I'm hooked my friend
To the boy who makes slaves out of men.
And oh believe me
Flying high in a friendly sky
Oh baby, flying high. "Flying high (In the Friendly Sky)" - Marvin Gaye 1972

My substance abuse escalated in my early teens. I dropped out of high school at fifteen to pursue my love affair with alcohol, drugs and the streets. The era of the 1960's changed the landscape of our nation as well as landscape of my heart. The Civil Rights Movement, the Hippie

Movement, the Black Power Movement, the Vietnam War, the proliferation of illegal drugs, integration, the assassinations of John F. Kennedy, Malcolm X, and Martin Luther King Jr. and Robert Kennedy all combined to heighten my social awareness and shape my worldview.

The Motown sound dominated the airwaves as we bopped and slow danced to Smokey Robinson, The Temptations, and The Four Tops among others. The Memphis sound gave us Al Green, Rufus Thomas and Isaac Hayes while Philadelphia pumped out soulful hits from the O-Jays, the Delphonics and Teddy Pendergrass. I cannot forget the Dells, Chi-Lites and the Blues greats Howling Wolf, Buddy Guy and Muddy Waters, from Chicago. My daddy loved the Blues and passed that love to my brother and me. I related to the O'Jay's hit of the 70's, *"I Love Music."* I loved music, any kind of music but when the jukebox stopped and party lights dimmed, the misery returned.

I developed a bulletproof emotional shell to protect me from my pain. I fortified it with drugs and alcohol. This strategy failed because when I came down off my high the pain returned. Addicts call this chasing a ghost because permanent relief from your pain eludes you. You chase that first feeling of euphoria repeatedly and never find it. King Solomon in Ecclesiastes said, *"This also is vanity and grasping for the wind (Ecclesiastes 2:26b NKJV)."*

By that time, my father stopped drinking. After an accident at work, doctors diagnosed him with cirrhosis of the liver. They told him that if he continued drinking, he would die. He stopped drinking and remained sober for 23 years, until his death in 1987 from liver cancer. To his credit, after he sobered up, he treated my mother like a queen. She stood by him through his hard times and he reciprocated by becoming the model husband. He seldom raised his voice and made sure she received her hearts desire. She paid her dues, hung in the marriage and reaped the benefits during the autumn and winter of her life. She exemplified a longsuffering rarely seen in marriages today.

He tried to make up for lost time in his and my relationship but, by that time, the streets possessed me. In addition, I needed someone to blame for my misery and he provided the perfect scapegoat. I used blame to avoid responsibility for my behavior and he, along with society, provided the perfect scapegoats.

My father gave up trying to discipline me and in 1967, committed me to the care of the Illinois Youth Commission. He hoped that the State could help me. He knew death awaited me if I continued courting the streets. The night before he had me committed, I came home hallucinating and talking out of my head. My friends and I, earlier that day experimented with some drugs similar to LSD that totally sent me on a bad trip. I failed to recognize my girlfriend, Marilyn as she walked me home. I talked to tree stumps and friends who were not there. When I arrived home, I asked my mother for a cigarette because I did not recognize her. I mistook my room for the park and started talking to my imaginary friends again. This alarmed my father. He thought I totally lost my mind from so much substance abuse. The next morning, I had a court date for some juvenile offense when my father told the judge, "your honor, I cannot do anything with Alfred, please lock him up so he can receive some help."

The State deemed me incorrigible and sent me to reform school in St. Charles, Illinois, which housed some of the most delinquent youth and gang members in Illinois. St. Charles consisted of about twenty-two houses or cottages, with about forty boys in each cottage. Each cottage was named after a president. House parents ran the cottages and they sectioned us off according to size and the seriousness of our crime. I lived in Taylor and Adams, which consisted of the intermediate sized boys about fifteen years old.

One morning, as we lined up to go to work and/or school, I got into a confrontation with a person in my cottage named Grant. I shadow boxed behind him in line, tapping him on the back. He asked me to stop and I ignored him. He turned around and punched me in my chest. The room became silent as everyone watched the drama unfold. I faced two choices: ignore it to stay out of trouble and obtain the label of a punk or retaliate and face the possibility of going to the hole and receiving a setback, which meant more time. I chose to retaliate because the last thing you want in jail is to carry the label of a punk.

The house parent read my thoughts as we left the cottage. He begged me not to retaliate but he knew the dilemma I faced. I raced before this boy to the school building and hid behind a stairwell. I waited until he walked up the steps and pounced on him. I pounded him until someone stopped the fight. I put him in the hospital with a punch to his eye. The superintendent sentenced me to the hole until the hospital released the boy. I stayed in the hole three days. I missed my Christmas visit with my parents but my reputation at the institution remained solid. I did not have any trouble after that. I avoided violence which caused people to underestimate me however, when cornered I responded like a ghetto alley rat and surprised people with the intensity of my anger.

I read a lot in St. Charles and kept to myself. I inherited my love of reading from my mother. I read Claude Brown's *"Man Child in the Promise Land"* and *"The Autobiography of Malcolm X"*. I read Eldridge Cleaver's *"Soul on Ice."* I loved these books because the authors grew up in the streets and their militant philosophies appealed to me. These books kindled an ember of hope in my heart and ignited a desire to change society. I did not understand Martin Luther King's philosophy of non-violence. I related to Jamil Abdullah al-amin (H.Rap Brown) when he shouted "Burn Baby Burn!" I shouted amen when Kwame Ture (Stokely Carmichael) raised his fist and screamed "Black Power!" I developed an impotent militancy that failed to produce any social change and I turned my social awareness into another excuse to get high. I added racism to my files of blame and developed a victim's mentality that stunted the growth in my life. Instead of helping to solve society's problems, I became a problem.

In April 1968, James Earl Ray assassinated Martin Luther King's Jr. Martin Luther King Jr. espoused the philosophy of non-violence yet violence snuffed his life out at the young age of thirty-nine. At St. Charles, we saw the news on T.V. King's death reinforced my anger and cynicism against society. His death added another brick to the stronghold of pessimism building in my mind. I suppressed these intense emotions and cloaked them with a carefree attitude. I reinforced my emotional shell to protect my sensitivity and sanity. The singing group War sang a song during that period that said:

"Slippin into darkness
Take my mind beyond the dreams
I was slippin into darkness
Take my mind beyond the dreams . . .
You been slippin into darkness
Pretty soon you gonna pay." I paid!

IYC (Illinois Youth Commission) paroled me in August of 1968. Edwin Hawkins and the Hawkins Family released their first hit *"O Happy Day."* I sang it when I walked out of those gates. I could not wait to go back to 79th street and my friends. I packed away my newfound social consciousness and hit the block as if I never left. I stayed out of jail about six months before the State incarcerated me again. In all, I spent 16 months in the juvenile reform system.

While incarcerated my girlfriend Wanda, gave birth to my first daughter Lisa. I hid this from my parents for two years.

I introduced Lisa to my parents when she was two. I can still remember the disbelief and shock on their faces when I introduced her to them. Lisa resembled me in everyway, so that did not produce the shock. The disbelief and shock came from realizing I could hide something this big from them for so long.

I lacked the maturity to father Lisa. My emotional issues overshadowed my feeble attempts at fatherhood. I would pick Lisa up from her mothers' house and take her with me to hang out on 79th street. Imagine this little girl, all dressed up hanging out with dope fiends and thugs. The liquor store clerks on 79th street knew Lisa because she accompanied me on my many visits to their establishments.

I started taking Lisa home late, after I became drunk, and her mother stopped letting me take her away from their house. I did my best to embrace fatherhood, which amounted to almost nothing. My selfish lifestyle kept me from helping to raise my daughter and caused a split between Lisa and I. We later worked out some major issues in our relationship and today, we enjoy a close relationship despite my lack of nurturing in her young life. Lisa overcame her unstable beginnings and achieved her Master's Degree from Syracuse University. She now counsels in the Chicago Public School system and blessed me with a beautiful granddaughter, Tyler. I am eternally grateful that God can heal any relationship.

Chapter 4

Babies and Fools

Remember dear brothers and sisters, that few of you were wise in the world's eyes, or powerful or wealthy when God called you. Instead God deliberately chose things the world considers foolish in order to shame those who think they are wise. And he chose those who are powerless to shame those who are powerful. So that no one can ever boast in the presence of the Lord (1Corinthians 1: 26, 27, 29 NLT).

Everybody plays the fool . . . sometimes "Everybody Plays The Fool" - The Main Ingredient 1972

At seventeen, I graduated to shooting heroin and prowled the streets like an animal. Like ravenous wolves, my friends and I preyed on any unsuspecting victim to support our drug habits. We lacked morals and did not respect the person or property of anyone. One evening as we roamed the streets we came upon a church service. We heard the music playing and the voices lifted in praise and decided to investigate. We walked in and took a seat in the back of the church. I sat behind a woman with her hands upraised and her eyes closed in praise. I saw my opportunity and stole her purse. My friend and I headed for the door, hotly pursued by the deacons who saw what went down. I ran a few blocks and tossed the purse over a fence, hoping to throw away the evidence. The deacons caught me, retrieved the purse and called the police. The police booked me and charged me with theft.

I went to court confident that these good church folks would not prosecute me. To my surprise, these church folk filled half of the courtroom. They testified and I received thirty days in the Chicago House of Correction. I graduated from the juvenile detention centers to the adult jails. This church exhibited some tough love, something I needed. I served my thirty days however; this did not stop my descent into degradation and addiction. Nevertheless, something deeper happened. I believe that church started praying for me! God wrapped his arms around me and started drawing me in! Sometimes, God allows us to hit rock bottom before we decide to look up. God heard their prayer but I needed some hard knocks to soften me and bring me to my knees.

It is a saying "God might not come when you want Him to, but He's always on time." It appeared that God took his time answering the churches prayer because I became worse. My cousin Tony and I worked for my father at the parking lot in downtown Chicago. Along with my mother, the gangsters stuck by my father through his drinking period and when he sobered up made him manager of one of their parking lots. He hired my cousin and me to work for him. We made good tips but squandered them every night drinking wine and shooting heroin. I ran many other side hustles while at work. We shot craps, stole out of the customers' cars and I conned some girls that worked in a cologne store to give me free cologne to sell. I borrowed money from loan sharks and jeopardized my life by refusing to pay them. I stole anything not tied down.

I begged, borrowed and stole to support my habits. Another old saying is, "God takes care of babies and fools." I left the baby stage but I qualified in the fool department.

I am going to fast forward to avoid redundancy. I eventually lost my job with my father for stealing money out of the cash register and wrecking a customer's car while drunk. At twenty-two, my parents put me out. Homeless, broke and needing a heroin fix - I went on a shoplifting spree. I would take orders for fresh meat raid the local grocery stores to fill the orders. Generally, I walked in, filled my shopping bag with stolen goods and walked out. This worked because I looked crazy and the clerks usually turned the other way as I walked past. However, this time the storeowners caught me. My crazy wild look did not intimidate them. Deep inside, I felt a wave of relief because I felt that finally I might find help.

To my surprise, instead of calling the police, the storeowners prayed for me. They refused to let my addiction intimidate them and stop them from carrying out God's purpose. Through the fog of drugs and alcohol, I vaguely remembered these storeowners. They told me the location of their church and the light bulb in my head lit up. They attended the church from where I stole the purse five years earlier. That church owned the grocery store! These same men chased and caught me then and now they apprehended me again. I know that church started praying for me then and God answered their prayer. Additionally, he allowed them to see the answer to their prayer. A couple of years later, God gave me an opportunity to meet the woman whose purse I stole and share my testimony on the church's weekly broadcast.

After praying for me, the storeowners took me to a Christian drug program called Teen Challenge, which specialized in helping street addicts. In my first week at Teen Challenge, on January 4, 1975, I accepted Jesus Christ as my personal Savior! Halleluiah, my spiritual journey began! During my time at Teen Challenge, God restored my physical and mental health through a strict regiment of Bible study, church attendance and prayer. They also moved us out of the city to a farm near Cape Girardeau, MO, over 400 miles away from Chicago. I remained at Teen Challenge for a year.

Teen Challenge helped me focus on God without the distractions of the streets. We attended Bible study during the morning and worked the farm or went to school in the afternoon. In the evening, we went to church. I am forever grateful to God for delivering me when He did! While away at Teen Challenge, a drug scourge engulfed my old neighborhood and many friends started dying from heroin overdoses.

One of those fatalities, my first cousin Tony, hit me extremely hard. I started him shooting heroin and many people said I should be the one dead. I loved him like a brother and his death sealed my plans to leave the streets of Chicago, for good. Tony died at twenty-three. I still remember how we talked about not living past thirty years old. Tony wrote his epitaph.

Chapter 5

Tricked, Bamboozled and Hoodwinked

∞

But I am not surprised! Even Satan can disguise himself as an angel of light (2corinthinthians 11:14 NLT).

How do you mend a broken heart?
How can a loser ever win? – Al Green

Upon graduation, Teen Challenge offered me an opportunity to work as a drug counselor. They gave me the choice of choosing between St. Louis and Pensacola, Florida, as cities to work in. Both cities offered me an opportunity to start over without the hindrance of so-called friends and familiar hangouts pulling at me to return to my old lifestyle. I chose St. Louis because of its closeness to Chicago and for its urban flavor. I arrived at the Union Station in St. Louis on a frosty, cold evening in January of 1976. During the cab ride from the train station, I witnessed that urban flavor first hand. Prostitutes lined Washington Boulevard on both sides of the street, hawking sex for sale. Teen Challenge - in the 5200 block of Washington Blvd. – bordered the prostitute stroll. I felt at home because I knew God called me to witness to prostitutes, drug addicts, pimps and other ne'er' do wells. He delivered me from this lifestyle and he expected me to share that message. The harvest looked ripe and I wanted to save the world!

I felt fantastic! God restored my life and loosened the chokehold drugs and alcohol had on my mind. Spiritual scales fell from my eyes and I saw my old lover – the streets – in her true form. Instead of a beautiful, alluring young woman with the promise of happiness and prestige, she looked like a toothless hag whose rank breath smelled from the bitter lives she consumed, as they fell into her bottomless pit of despair.

I anticipated a fresh start in a new city with endless possibilities. My old worldview changed as God illuminated my path by the transforming power of His Word. God sense replaced street sense. I counseled other recovering addicts and felt a newfound purpose for living that only comes from walking in God's will. My parents finally could brag about me and stop worrying that someone would find me dead in some back alley or dope den. I bought an old Rosetta Tharpe album that featured one of my favorite gospel songs, *"Up Above My Head I Hear Music."* I played this song daily with James Cleveland's, *"Jesus Is the Best Thing That Ever Happened To Me"*, and acquainted myself with St. Louis.

I gave my testimony at Assembly of God Churches around the city and state. I traveled with the director of Teen Challenge as we raised funds for the program. Teen Challenge did not receive state funds and ran its' houses from donations. This enabled them to run the program without the interference and mindless bureaucracy of the state. God honed my speaking skills at these churches. I lacked the loquaciousness and outgoing gregariousness that came naturally to my father and brother. Like Moses, I needed help overcoming my reluctance to speak. Naturally shy and reserved, I preferred to study God's Word instead of speaking. However, congregations enthusiastically received my testimony, because of the anointing of the Holy Spirit, and my confidence as a speaker improved.

I found a church home around the corner from Teen Challenge, in the 5200 block of Delmar, called the Prayer Garden Church of God In Christ. A storefront, the Prayer Garden lacked a beautiful building, but abounded in spiritual fervor. We conducted church almost every night sometimes until midnight and beyond. Elder Norman C. Pitt shepherded the flock at the Prayer Garden as he preached fire and brimstone, holiness or hell. I cut my spiritual teeth at the Prayer Garden and grew into my calling. I looked forward to testimony service where I could express how the Lord showed me revelations in his Word. Once shy and reluctant to speak, I now looked forward to sharing God's Word. In 1977, I accepted my calling to preach and Elder Pitt officially ordained me in April of 1978. I became an Elder in the Church of God in Christ. At the Prayer Garden, I learned the importance of paying tithes and giving to God's work. I tithed on the insignificant salary I made at Teen Challenge and God provided for my every need. I topped out at fifteen dollars per week at Teen Challenge, because they provided food and housing, but those remain some of the spiritually richest days of my life.

Young and virile, I started looking for a wife. The Prayer Garden offered a variety of beautiful, young saved sisters from which to choose. I really did not have much to offer besides good intentions but my flesh burned and I could not see past my passion. I needed to get some spiritual maturity before I married anyone. I never ran a household or even paid a bill. I abounded in street experience but fell short in the practical living department.

I disregarded the red flags the Holy Spirit threw up telling me to allow God to mature me emotionally, spiritually and financially before I married anyone. I became like King Saul. In (**1Samuel 15**), God commanded Saul to kill all the Amalekites. He told him to kill man and woman, infant and suckling, ox and sheep, camel and ass (**1Samuel 15:3**). Saul disobeyed God and spared Agag, the king, and the best sheep, oxen lambs and all that was good (**1Samuel 15:9**). When confronted with his disobedience, by the prophet Samuel, Saul rationalized his disobedience by saying he spared the best to offer to God. Like Saul, I did not mind killing the vile things like drugs and alcohol because of the misery they caused in my life. However, I wanted to keep some of the "best" things. I wanted to keep my self-will.

In addition, like King Saul, I camouflaged my rebellion with religious works (**1Samuel 15:22, 23**) and used scripture to justify my decision. I used (**1Corinthians 7:9**) that says if you cannot exercise self-control then it is better to marry than to burn up with passion. Saul paid a hefty price for his rebellion. He lost his kingdom. My rebellion robbed me of the peace that comes from fellowship with God.

I met my first wife, Bernice at the Prayer Garden. We enjoyed a brief courtship and married in 1977. She conceived my first son Alfred Jr. on 12/21/1977. Bernice had two sons from a previous marriage, whom I adopted as my own. When we first met, Bernice and I would talk for hours about the Word and our past lives. Bernice grew up in the Pruitt Igoe projects and understood where I came from. She loved studying God's Word – as I did - and we compared notes and revelations from the Word. I admired Bernice's strength and leadership abilities. She came from a large family and they looked to her for leadership.

Her family immediately accepted me and included me in family functions. This meant a lot to me because I came from a small family and our dysfunction kept us distant from one another. We fell in love and married.

After the honeymoon, reality kicked in and we started clashing. God uses marriage to mold both partners into His image. As King Solomon said, *"As iron sharpeneth iron, a friend sharpens a friend (Proverbs 27:17).* He uses the clashes to bring us to our knees and then back into each other's arms. The Bible teaches us to embrace our anger without sinning (**Ephesians 4:26**). When we allow anger to rest in our hearts, we start acting foolishly (**Psalm 37:8; Ecclesiastes 7:9**). Bernice and I, both independent and stubborn, would go days without speaking, then go to Church at night, and praise God. We allowed Satan to place a wedge in our marriage. Bernice needed a strong priest (**1Peter 2:9**) to help her raise the boys and head the household. I wanted a weak woman to spoil me and enable my insecurities. I loved Bernice, but struggled to step into my role as protector, provider and spiritual head of my household. I lacked maturity.

I struggled with anger and lust issues and my stormy relationship at home provided the perfect excuse to feel sorry for myself. Instead of becoming the priest in my household and demand that Bernice and I pray, to resolve our issues, I took a page from Adam. I blamed the woman God gave me (**Genesis 3:12**). Instead of allowing God to root out my pride and self-centeredness, I ran. I practiced the same behavior I exhibited as an addict. Run from your pain, go into denial, blame someone else for your issues and find something besides God to ease your hurt. Exercise stepped in as my new drug of choice.

I started exercising at Teen Challenge. After work or school, we ran a couple of miles before dinner as part of our recovery. Where other people dreaded running, I enjoyed it. During my six months of high school, I ran cross country and moved up to number one on the team before they expelled me for stealing out of my teammates lockers. I continued my workouts after I left Teen Challenge and especially loved jogging because it provided me the solitary time to clear my head and gave me the benefit of a strong heart. I used running and working out as an escape valve to let off steam. I literally ran – physically and emotionally - from my issues at home. I increased my weekly running mileage to about fifty miles per week. In 1981, I completed two 26.1-mile marathon races with some decent times. I loved running!

I also enjoyed the social portion that surrounded running. When runners strip to their running gear, everyone becomes equal. Running shorts replaced doctor's smocks and lawyer's suits. The CEO of the Fortune 500 Company ran alongside the ex-addict with running as the common denominator that linked us. Like drugs and alcohol, running felt good and temporarily satisfied some of my needs. I became addicted to running which, at the time, looked harmless. The enemy hoodwinked, bamboozled and tricked me into opening the door to another addiction.

William Glasser, M.D. in his 1976 book *"Positive Addiction",* described running as a positive addiction. He said, *"To become "addicted" to positive behavior – for instance, running or meditating, or some other activity performed for a specific period each day. These positive addictions – contrary to negative addictions to drugs, alcohol, smoking, overeating or excessive caffeine – can strengthen a person so he or she can overcome such negative addictions and lead a more integrated and rewarding life."*
[1] *I* believed this worldly philosophy. Paul said in his Epistle to the Colossians, *"Don't let anyone lead you astray with empty philosophy and high sounding nonsense that come from human thinking and from the evil powers of this world and not from Christ (Colossians 2:8 (NLT).*

The Bible says that we become slaves of anything we allow to control us – besides God **(Romans 6:16)** – negative or positive. It also said that Satan can masquerade as an angel of light **(2Corinthians 11:14).** He uses the same tactics he used on Eve in the Garden. As they say in the streets, "The game stays the same, just the players' change." Running looked good, it made me feel good and I met some influential people through running - the lust of the eye, the lust of the flesh, and pride of life **(Genesis 3:1 -13; 1John 2:16; 2Corinthians 11:14)**. Running became the perfect substitute for drugs and alcohol. Satan used deception to disguise his true motives. Though innocent and sweet looking, this "positive addiction" seduced me, and like a prostitute on the stroll, set me up for her evil friends lurking in the shadows to steal my joy, fellowship with God and my reputation.

I raced every weekend and started missing church. My running program overshadowed my personal devotions. I rationalized that the church is in my heart and I did not need to worship God in the physical building. I could worship Him on the run. I disregarded **(Hebrews 10:25)** that commands us to attend church regularly, for exhortation and accountability to the Body of Christ. Every flaw in the church became noticeable to me. I felt that the running community understood me more than the church community did. My spiritual foundation started crumbling and I became ripe for a fall. I neglected my marriage and it eventually unraveled, along with the rest of my life.

Chapter 6

Broken Clay
~~~

The Lord gave another message to Jeremiah. He said, "Go down to the shop where clay pots and jars are made. I will speak to you while you are there." So I did as He told me and found the potter working at his wheel. But the jar he was making did not turn out as he had hoped, so the potter squashed the jar into a lump of clay and started again. Then the Lord gave me this message: "O Israel, can I not do to you as this potter has done to his clay? As the clay is in the potter's hand, so are you in my hand (Jeremiah 1:1 – 6 NLT)."

God blessed me with several jobs during this period and I settled at The Emergency Children's Home (ECHO). I worked at ECHO from 1978 to 1984 – my longest tenure at any job. ECHO provided shelter for abused children and I enjoyed working there because I wanted to make a difference in these children's lives. I understood them on many levels and they could sense my compassion. Working at ECHO fulfilled my need to feel worthy and provided an escape from my problems at home. If I engrossed myself in my job and the needs of the children, I could evade my own issues. I rose to the rank of Senior Child Care Worker, overseeing the two buildings that housed the boys. I became a workaholic. After a major blizzard in 1982, I actually ran to work. Public Transportation halted because of the snow and most streets were impassable. I combined my two new "harmless" addictions, running, work, and was the only worker to show up that day.

I resigned from ECHO in 1984 and started driving a cab. After a disagreement with my direct supervisor, I gave him my two-week resignation notice. I felt that the organization showed more concern for the physical grounds than they did for the children. I left on principle and told my supervisor I would drive a cab before I submitted to their policies. I made good on my word. I loved driving a cab because of the freedom to make my own hours. I worked the 4 p.m. to 4 a.m. shift so I caught all the night action. My old lover –the streets – like Jezebel in (**2Kings 9:30**) - fixed her hair, painted her eyes and started flirting with me again. I forgot how she hurt me in the past and her murderous ways and flirted back. I started enjoying the nightlife again.

One Sunday afternoon, at the Prayer Garden, I preached a message "What's Love Got to Do With It." I borrowed the title from Tina Turner's hit song of the same title. God anointed the message and I felt good about it. I went to work that afternoon and while waiting for a fare, a young woman jumped in the front seat of the cab. I thought she called the cab. I asked her destination and she simply said, "With you!" I entertained the temptation and fell to her wiles. I allowed the enemy to steal my victory and reputation. The Bible teaches us to flee from fornication (**1Corinthians 6:18**). Joseph ran from it (**Genesis39:1 -17**) however, I ran to it. After I fell, I allowed Satan to heap condemnation on me. I convinced myself that to return to the pulpit would mark me as a hypocrite.

My pride kept me from receiving God's forgiveness and returning to the race (**1John 1:9**). I did not preach again at a church until almost 20 years later when my current pastor, Dr F. James Clark allowed me to preach at the Shalom Church (City of Peace).

Physically strong and spiritually weak, I left the church and pursued the world. I started drinking again and engaged in several adulterous affairs. Bernice after countless attempts at reconciliation sought some counsel from my mother. My parents loved and respected Bernice. My mother told her, "Baby leave while you can, you do not want to see Alfred in that state." Bernice - tired of my shenanigans – finally packed my bags and left them on the back porch for me to pick up after work. We eventually divorced and to her credit always allowed me to spend time with my son. We eventually patched up our differences, today enjoy a close friendship, and shared ministry. God called Bernice to Pastor and she is a blessing to me in many ways. She exemplifies strength and spirituality refined in the furnace of suffering – some of which I caused.

However, like a marred piece of pottery on the potters' wheel, I needed breaking so God could remold me and shape me into a vessel of honor (**Jeremiah 18:1-8**). God chastens us to bring us back into fellowship with Himself because he is committed to our maturity as his children (**Philippians 1:6; Hebrews 12:5 – 11**). God's chastening hurts but is necessary for our spiritual growth. It is like the saying, "A hard head makes a soft behind."

Like the father in the parable of the Prodigal Son, God allowed me to take my inheritance and go to the far country – in my case the world and its accompanying evil (**Luke 15:11 – 32**). Just like the snake suggested to Eve that God was withholding something good from her, I felt that I needed freedom to explore the world without the restrictions of the church (**Genesis 3:4, 5**).

After driving the cab for a few months, one of Bernice's nephews told me about a job opportunity at General Motors. They just completed building a new plant in Wentzville, Missouri and needed to hire a night shift. I passed all the requirements and they hired me in May of 1984. I gave up my cab to work at General Motors. I made more money than I had ever made in life and had full benefits! In 1984, the Commodores had a hit called; *"Night Shift"* and that became our theme song. My drinking increased as I adjusted to life on the assembly line. I tried to fool myself into thinking I could handle drinking wine and beer. I knew better but my denial canceled any common sense. I spiraled downward, slowly at first but the descent gained momentum.

I met my second wife Denise, in 1984, at Vic Tanny's, now called Bally's Health Club. We shared a love for physical fitness and often ran and took aerobic classes together. I loved aerobic dance because of the music and women in the class. Most times, I would be the only man in the classes. I felt like a rooster in a hen house. Eventually, Denise and I started dating, and when I separated from Bernice, I moved in with Denise. She became pregnant and conceived my youngest daughter, Tamar, October 16, 1986.

She introduced me to another side of life. She only shopped at the finest stores and had a sharp mind for business. She knew how to save and budget her money. On the other hand, I wasted money and this caused enormous friction between us. Strong and independent, I did not understand what she saw in me. She later told me that she saw God's light in my life. Like a moth to the fire, God's light attracted her to me. God kept my shining despite my backslidings and my attempt to run from his presence. David said, *"I can never escape from your Spirit! I can never get away from your presence! If I go up to heaven, you are there; if I go down to the place of the dead, you are there. If I ride the wings of the morning, if I dwell by the farthest oceans, even there your hand will guide me and your strength will support me. I could ask the darkness to hide me and the light around me to become night but even in darkness, I cannot hide from you. To you the night shines as bright as day. Darkness and light are both alike to you (Psalm 139:7 -12 NLT).*

Backsliders carry an enormous amount of guilt and shame because they know the truth and decide to pursue other gods that do not satisfy. Life becomes hard as God's chastening increases.

Denise and I shacked for about five years until she started describing to me some spiritual stirrings she felt. I recognized the move of the Holy Spirit in her life. He desired to draw her to salvation and I did not want to block the movement of God. I took Denise to church and she accepted Christ in her life. I married her to keep her from living in sin.

Again, I ran from my duty as priest over my household. I sent Denise to church instead of repenting and returning to church myself. Without my support, her faith weakened and our issues increased. I took my guilt and shame out on Denise and periodically exploded in angry tirades like those that my father had during my childhood. She grew tired of the madness and we eventually separated and divorced. We remained friends and eventually became members together at the Shalom Church (City of Peace). God strengthened her faith through the strong, anointed preaching of Pastor Clark and she became a spiritual example to her family and friends.

Denise, though extremely strong and healthy contracted a rare disease called POEMS. Her shapely, strong body deteriorated but her spirit remained strong. She felt great pain in the last two years of her life but never cursed God. She stayed in her Word until she became too weak to hold a Bible. She then listened to the Word on tapes and CD's. She died at 52, in 2006. She entered glory like a soldier!

Chapter 7

The Long Way Home
∞

So he returned home to his father. And while he was still a long distance away, his father saw him coming. Filled with love and compassion, he ran to his son, embraced him and kissed him. But his father said to the servants, "Quick bring the finest robe in the house and put it on him. Get a ring for his finger, and sandals for his feet. And kill the calf we have been fattening in the pen. We must celebrate with a feast, for this son of mine was dead and has now returned to life. He was lost and now he is found. So the party began (Luke 15:20, 22–24 NLT).

There are some things, I may not know
There are some places I can't go
But I am sure of this one thing
My God is real for I can feel him in my soul – Church hymn

God allowed me to experience everything I thought would make me happy. I had a good job, I graduated from college with a degree in electronics, I married again, and I socialized with influential people, yet I was miserable.

At this point, God systematically and strategically dismantled all of my strongholds (**2Corinthians 10:3–5**). He took away all my crutches to force me to lean on him.

I entered my first secular recovery program in 1987. Laid off at General Motors, I decided to get a degree in Electronics Engineering Technology. However, I drank a 40 ounce of Colt 45 malt liquor every morning before school. I realized after the first two weeks, that school and drinking did not mix. I decided to check myself into an in-patient rehab program at Central Hospital. I stayed for 12 days and left the program without finishing. I finished school with my degree and stayed clean for five years until an accident at work left me in much physical pain.

One afternoon while playing softball, on the company team, I slid into second base. I injured my right hip with a hairline stress fracture that went undiagnosed for years. This accident also ended my running career. At work, I obtained Darvocets – a painkiller – to make it through the night. Not only did the Darvocets ease the pain, they made me high. My tolerance for these pills grew daily. Before breakfast, I took eight Darvocet and four Xanax pills. I masked my addiction to pain pills by obtaining legal prescriptions from as many as six doctors at a time. It got to where pharmacies refused to fill my prescriptions. This forced me to step down my addiction to prescription drugs however, the drinking started back.

General Motors offered me a $100,000 buyout and I took it. I hated working on the assembly line and could not envision myself working thirty years mindlessly placing parts on vehicles. With the buy-out money, I planned to pursue my degree in Biomedical Engineering. This plan derailed after some teen-age gang members assaulted me in my cab, for a gang initiation.

I had resumed my cab-driving career to allow myself the flexibility to finish school and because I liked to drive cabs.

I planned to buy three or four cabs and start a small business to bankroll my plans.

One sunny Saturday afternoon in July of 1994 while driving my cab, I picked up two teen-age boys. Denise hated and feared my driving a cab because of the danger. I ignored her warnings because I felt I knew the streets enough to ward off any danger. However, something was different about these boys. Red flags flew up everywhere. Number one, they did not enter the cab from the store address they gave the dispatcher. They came from across the street near the housing projects. Number two, they looked suspicious.

They gave me an address and I noticed how nervous they looked. I turned around to get a good look at them and the hairs stood on the back of my neck. One boy, the leader, had the coldest most hate-filled eyes I ever seen. They reminded me of snake eyes. The other boy looked stealthy as if he was up to something. Instinctively, I planned for trouble.

I could not reach my pistol while driving because earlier I locked it in my glove compartment because I did not anticipate any trouble in midday of a Saturday. The boys started an argument with me about the route I took to get them to their destination. They conjured up enough anger to give them courage for their evil intentions. I recognized this tactic from my days on the street. You prepared yourself to commit a crime by dehumanizing your victim. You became angry for no reason to numb your conscious and make the crime easier to commit. I instantly devised a strategy if anything went down. I planned to place the cab in drive and jump out, leaving the boys to roll down the street in the opposite direction.

I arrived at their destination and informed them of their fare. I felt a heavy thud on the back of my neck. I thought they hit me with a club or something. Everything seemed like a surreal slow motion scene out of a movie. I followed my plan and placed the cab in drive as they hit me three more times. As I ran, I noticed my white shirt turn red from blood but still did not know the extent of my injuries. I ran to a barbershop. God blessed me with the presence of mind to run to a brightly lit business with plenty of people, in case the boys gave chase and caught me. The barbers and patrons in the shop took one look at my wounds and called the police. I still thought the boys clubbed me until one of the barbers told me I was stabbed. The police came and questioned me. I begged them to find the cab before these boys found my pistol in the glove compartment. I guess they did not feel the same urgency I felt. The found the cab later that evening with the gun missing.

While watching the news from the hospital Sunday evening, I saw where a cab driver was shot and killed in the same neighborhood of my attack. I knew in my spirit that the same boys that stabbed me killed this other cab driver. In addition, they probably used my gun. My premonition proved correct. I provided the police with some empty shells from my gun to run some tests. The tests proved that my gun killed this other cab driver. I identified one boy in a line up and the other boy's grandmother turned him in. I later found out that a stupid gang initiation provoked this killing. The gang required new members to kill an innocent victim for admission to the gang. A seasoned gang member verified the killing and sponsored the new member. The boy with the cold eyes confirmed the killing because he already achieved his rank in the gang.

Two weeks before his death, the slain cab driver joined church and accepted Jesus Christ as his personal Savior. God called him to glory but still had plans for me.

After the stabbing, I left school because my brain could not handle the Calculus and Advanced Biology classes. For the first time in my life, schoolwork became hard. I made a half-hearted effort to renew my fellowship with God. I joined Transformation Church under the leadership of Bishop Richard Burruss and his wife Pastor Priscellius Burrus. Bishop Burruss reigned during the 1960's and early 70's as one of the kingpins in the dope dealing traffic in St. Louis. God saved him and he founded his church with ex-addicts, prostitutes, alcoholics and thieves. He preached a no nonsense Gospel that appealed to hard-core people from the streets. I joined Transformation's Prison Ministry but again I used religious works to camouflage my rebellion. I met the father of one of the young men responsible for my stabbing at Transformation. It shocked him to find out his son stabbed me. We both preached at the prisons and shared similar backgrounds. God allowed me to forgive his son and I asked his father to relay that message. I recently spoke with the father to offer him condolences for the death of his wife. He informed me that his son accepted the Lord in prison and married the niece of Bishop Burrus. That is Amazing Grace! As for me, I had not totally submitted to God and needed more chastening.

Like a snowball rolling down the side of a mountain, my decline gained momentum. Denise and I separated; I gained and lost several jobs; I lived in a dump and drank heavily. I resumed driving a cab and my world shrank to little more than drinking and driving. I started a relationship with a young woman named Sharon. I entered that relationship with enough baggage to fill an airport turnstile. Sharon possessed a quiet, sweet personality but I became possessive, paranoid and extremely jealous for no reason. Eventually she tired of my senseless tirades and accusations and ended the relationship. Sharon and I eventually resumed our relationship and remain friends to this day.

All the years of denial and running from God wore me down. I could not maintain a sane relationship or even hold a decent job. To drown my sorrow and feed my self-pity, I drank myself senseless one night. I awoke after about one hour of sleep. The cab company contracted with the Board of Education to provide transportation for children to get to and from school. These lucrative routes provided guaranteed money without having to hustle fares all day. I did not want to lose this easy money so I forced myself to drive. The roads were slick from an overnight ice and snowstorm. I rushed out still drunk from the night before and crashed head-on into another vehicle. I broke my nose and wrist, in the accident and seriously injured the passengers in the other car. I remember the horrific sound of metal against metal and the sound of glass shattering. I also remember hearing a small, still voice, through the deafening noise, tell me "This is it, it is time for surrender." Like the prodigal son in **(Luke 15:11–32),** I came to myself.

I lost everything; job, woman, car, and home. I faced possible charges for drunk driving that could carry a jail sentence. I descended downward about as far as I could go without dying, when my spirit reminded me, "You can go home." I finally surrendered and God stood waiting for me with open arms! In fact, he never left me; I left him **(Hebrews 13:5).** I remembered the peace of mind I enjoyed in God's presence and compared it to the misery I now felt. I exchanged the pig slop, of the world, for the fatted calf God offered at his table.

When I left the hospital, I reported to the outpatient drug program I attended named BASIC. BASIC, founded by Oval Miller Sr., provided outpatient drug treatment services targeting the African-American community. I went to group sessions two times a week where we discussed our substance abuse issues. I drank throughout my treatment, sobering up just long enough to attend my sessions as I tried desperately to hide my deception. I did not fool anyone but myself. BASIC welcomed me back into a nurturing forgiving environment and recommended that I enter an in house treatment program because of the severity of my problem. Oval Miller Jr., son of the director, helped me pack my few belongings and made sure I honored my commitment to seek treatment. He drove me to the Agape House.

The Agape House is an in-house Christian drug and alcohol treatment program. The Reverend James Potter is the founder and director of this program. The Agape House offered a hard-core Christian curriculum that weeded out pretenders within the first week of entering the program. From sun up to sun down Reverend Potter and his staff engaged us in bible study, prayer and church services. Rev. Potter housed the program in a run down house on Tower Grove Ave., in the heart of the city. Rev. Potter did not receive any state money and donors gave us everything. I bunked with other addicts, sometimes four to a room. I slept on the top bunk, which presented a major challenge, because I had a rod in my arm from the car accident.

You could not fake it at the Agape House. Reverend Potter spotted phonies quickly and. he believed in tough love. He discerned if you needed some more hard knocks and would not hesitate to expel you from the program. I graduated from the Agape House in April of 1998. I needed that spiritual boot camp to ground me back in God's Word.

My journey took a full circle. I entered salvation homeless and broke. I rebelled against God, found myself homeless and broke once more. Like the children of Israel, I wandered for years in the wilderness because of my rebelliousness. I tried things my way and made a shambles of my life. When I finally surrendered, God quickly restored the years I lost **(Joel 2:25)**.

After leaving the Agape House, I worked as a telemarketer for a few months until AT&T hired me. I quickly rose through the ranks. After sixteen months, I received a promotion to manager and after three years, I received another promotion to second level management. This usually takes 20 or more years with the company. I did it in four.

I joined the Shalom Church (City of Peace), under the leadership of Dr F. James Clark in 1998 and serve as an Associate Minister. Pastor Clark amazes me Sunday after Sunday with his Spirit-led preaching and teaching. I heard Pastor Clark preach for the first time, right before I entered the Agape House. After that sermon, I knew I had to sit under his leadership. I vowed when I joined Shalom, that the running away from pain is over. Come hell or high water, I am staying until God says different. At the age of 55, I feel that I have finally grown up emotionally and spiritually so that God can use me to fulfill His original purpose for me; taking His Word to other suffering souls (**1Corinthians 13:11**).

My victory depends on my relationship with my Father. Paul said, *"If you think you are standing strong, be careful, for you, too, may fall into the same sin* ((**1Corinthians 10:12 NLT**). God deserves all the glory, in my life. I wrote this to offer myself as an example of God's grace and mercy. If God delivered me, He will deliver anyone! My spiritual scars and the limp I have from years of wrestling with God daily remind me of my frailties. I still struggle with many issues but this time, I am staying home. Like Paul, I have not yet attained but, I am pressing forward (**Philippians 3:12–14**).

My program to maintain sobriety is a daily time of communion with God. I start everyday meditating in Gods Word. I ask for my daily portion of strength and wisdom to make it one day at a time. I put the same rigor around my solitary time with God as I did pursuing my idols. I reject any condemnation or shame the enemy throws at me, realizing that Jesus died for my frailties and I can receive forgiveness because of his shed blood (**Romans 8:1**).

On Sunday 1/27/08, Pastor Clark preached about the call of Moses in (**Exodus 3:1-6, 14**). Though Moses tended sheep for 40 years on the backside of the desert – after he fled Egypt - God's invisible Hand still controlled the events of his life. God taught Moses to trust Him, in the desert, and developed humility in his heart, which he lacked as an Egyptian noble. It took years of isolation desolation, degradation and humiliation before Moses was ready to assume his position as leader of the children of Israel. I see similarities in my own life story. After years of running and rebelling, I see God's hands of love, breaking and then blessing my life. It worked for my good **(Romans 8:28)**. I remember my sermon from 1984, "What's Love Got To Do With It;" now I know!

Part 2

Working It Out

Dearest friends, you were always so careful to follow my instructions when I was with you. And now you must be even more careful to put into action god's saving work in your lives, obeying God with deep reverence and fear. For God is working in you, giving you the desire to obey him and the power to do what pleases him (Philippians 2:12, 13 NLT).

Chapter 1

From Dysfunction To God's Function

⦵

Do not copy the behavior and customs of this world, but let God transform you into a new person by changing the way you think. Then you will know what God wants you to do and you will know how good and pleasing and perfect his will really is (Romans 12:2 NLT).

My intention – with this study - is not to provide magic solutions to complex problems.

God's Word can and will transform our minds (**Romans 12:2**) as we face the truth about our spiritual, emotional and physical condition (**John 8:32**).

God calls this process Sanctification. He initiates it after Salvation to make us function right and to form us in the image of Christ (**2Timothy 1:6; Romans 8:29**). God empowers us with a practical theology, using scripture, to destroy the strongholds of addictions whatever they are.

In this study, we will expose some root causes of addictions and apply the healing balm of God's Word to the sick areas in our life (**2Kings 19:30; Isaiah 37:31; 53:5; 61:1**).

Sin underlies all addiction. We are born into sin not born into addiction **(Romans 5:12-14).**

Addictions are ultimately a disorder of worship. We usurp God's position as Lord of our lives and we replace Him with self. This reversal of roles is idolatry. The question is; will we worship our own desires and ourselves or will we worship the One and True God?

Our deliverance and spiritual freedom depend on our answer. [1]

God's purpose is that we live this life to the fullest without the encumbrances of a dysfunctional past **(John 10:10).** The *American Century Dictionary* defines dysfunction as an abnormality or impairment of functioning. I define it as functioning below the capacity God intended. When we function below God's intention, we miss God's purpose for our life. We squander our God-given talents, burying them in the ground of dysfunction and addiction.

Dysfunctional behavior starts in the family. Usually, an emotionally deprived family member disrupts the development of healthy behaviors and relationships of other family members. Everyone in the family focuses on that person. Usually, though not always, substance abuse leads the list of disruptive forces in a family. However, the list includes any addiction that tears at the foundation of love in a household.

All families experience problems. I grew up watching *"Father Knows Best"* and *"Leave It To Beaver"* where the father wears a tie at the dinner table and is always kind as he dispenses fair but firm discipline and wisdom to the family. Real life painted a different picture. Even the best families have faults and the worse families have strengths.

However, when the caretakers are chemically dependent or emotionally repressed, an underlying structure of disorder exists, in the family.

This damages other family members and they carry this damage into adulthood. Those family members develop dysfunctional behavior characteristics to cope with the disorder inherent in these families.

Like a wintry Chicago wind, coming off Lake Michigan, dysfunction can bend you over and make you walk crooked. Your worldview becomes distorted and abnormal becomes normal and normal appears abnormal. Your frame of reference consists only of your family and the daily drama you encounter as a member of that family. Without a positive example of how a "normal" family interacts, you accept dysfunction as a way of life. In the Gospel of Luke, Jesus encountered a woman bent over for eighteen years, caused by an evil spirit.

One Sabbath day as Jesus was teaching in a synagogue, He saw a woman who had been crippled by an evil spirit. She had been bent double for eighteen years and was unable to stand up straight. When Jesus saw her, He called her over and said "Woman, you are healed of your sickness!" Then He touched her and she could stand straight. How she praised and thanked God (Luke 13:10-13 NLT)!

The text says that Jesus saw her and called her over. He sought her out to heal her of her affliction. Can you imagine how much of life she missed bent over double, the pain she felt and the social stigma she encountered?

All of us exhibit some of the below characteristics at one time or another however they cause major problems in the adult lives of children from dysfunctional families. Let us examine some of these characteristics.

1. Characteristics of a Dysfunctional Family

    a. A dysfunctional family focuses its attention on an emotionally needy family member who usually has an addictive/compulsive personality. This person takes the place of God and family members develop the same root attitudes as the needy family member. The

Bible teaches us to focus on God and to give Him our undivided attention **(Hebrews 12:2; Colossians 3:2; Mark 12:30)**. God created us to live in this manner.

b. A dysfunctional family places limits on the expression of feelings. As a result, family members become out of touch with real feelings and live a life of denial. Our prayer lives are stifled and become ritualistic because it is hard to express our true feelings, even to God. God desires relationship with us and opened the door for us to express our innermost feelings with Him through prayer **(Matthew 6:5-8; Hebrews 4:15, 16)**.

c. A dysfunctional family discourages open talk about obvious problems. This hinders our spiritual growth because we avoid problems and conflict, as if they do not exist. This discourages honest dialog and precludes spiritual maturity and true Christian fellowship. We function as strong Christians when we trust God enough to lay all of our burdens at His feet. This helps us to help to other because we lose our fear of vulnerability **(James 5:16; 1John 1:7)**. This represents true fellowship. A dysfunctional family permits destructive roles for the children in the family. Children develop survival tactics and fall into roles that later in life turn into masks to cover up true feelings. Some roles learned in a dysfunctional family are:

  i. **The scapegoat** – parents may use the scapegoat child as someone to blame for the families problems.

  ii. **The lost child** – the lost child is present in the family but not present. Because of the persistent drama in a dysfunctional family, the lost child tries to become invisible to avoid conflict.

      iii. **The clown** – the clown is the child in the family who uses humor to lessen the tensions in the family.
      iv. **The hero** – the hero attempts to make the family look better by achieving success.
      v. **The rebel** – the rebel is always getting into trouble to make the family pay for their pain. The rebel follows one rule:" Don't follow the rules."
      vi. **The little parent** – the little parent makes up for the lack of parenting in the household by becoming a caretaker for one or more siblings. The loss of childhood is severe for this individual because they have no one to parent him or her.
      vii. **The little prince/princess** – this child can do no wrong. They become the family trophy to show that something good can come from this family. The other siblings usually resent them and they develop an inability to face their own limitations.
      viii. **The surrogate spouse** – this child becomes an emotional substitute for one of the parents. It may be limited to an emotional response however; it can also include sexual involvement.
      ix. **The placator** – this child is the fixer. They reduce conflict in the family by smoothing it over. [2]
d. A dysfunctional family fails to provide appropriate nurture for developing children. This hinders the ability to love and accept love, even God's love. As the child develops, into adulthood, it becomes almost impossible to trust and relationships suffer. Unresolved childhood issues rob us of the potential

God has deposited into our lives. A parent's main responsibility is to provide for the physical, emotional and spiritual needs of the children entrusted in their care **(Ephesians 6:4)**. Proper nurturing enables our children to function in society as well-adjusted productive citizens. Lack of this nurturing constitutes abuse.
e. A dysfunctional family closes itself to the outside world. Family members protect the family secret and live lives of denial. This hinders our worship of God because He demands that we worship Him in spirit and truth **(John 4:24)**. We become adept at "living a lie" and have trouble deciding what is real. God helps us to face our secrets. We have to "own them to disown them." Our deliverance comes when we become honest with God and ourselves about our secrets **(Psalm 139:23, 24)**. God sees our secrets and waits for us to confess them. [3]

2. Characteristics of Adults Reared in a Dysfunctional Family

a. Judgmental of self and others
b. Perfectionists
c. Controlling
d. Gossipers
e. Rebellious/problems with authority figures
f. Trouble accepting constructive criticism
g. Approval seekers
h. Live life as victims and are attracted to other victims
i. Overly responsible or very irresponsible
j. Passive and aggressive
k. Deny, minimize and repress feelings

l. Difficulty with intimate relationships/tend to chose emotionally unavailable people with addictive personalities, less attracted to healthy caring people
m. Lack of trust and no established boundaries in relationships
n. Will accept abuse in relationships because of fear of rejection or abandonment
o. Problems finishing projects
p. Procrastination
q. Impulsive
r. Isolation to avoid intimacy with other people especially authority figures
s. Problems developing a consistent prayer life
t. Church hoppers
u. Spiritual immaturity

Discovery Questions

What - if any - of the above characteristics do you exhibit on a regular basis?

What issues from your past continue to haunt you today?

What role did you play in your family of origin?

How is your relationship with God? Describe in detail.

What baggage from your dysfunctional past are you bringing into your relationship with God and other relationships? Be specific.

Chapter 2

Overcoming Abuse

The Spirit of the Sovereign Lord is upon me, because the Lord appointed me to bring good news to the poor. He has sent me to heal the brokenhearted and to announce that captives will be released and prisoners will be freed. He has sent me to tell those who mourn that the time of the lord's favor has come and with it, the day of God's anger against their enemies. To all who mourn in Israel, he will give beauty for ashes, joy instead of mourning, and praise instead of despair. For the Lord has planted them like strong and graceful oaks for his own glory (Isaiah 61:1 – 3 NLT).

I worked for six years at a home for abused children. It broke my heart to witness so much abuse of children. How could any adult inflict such pain on innocent children? Less obvious than the gross forms of sexual and physical abuse however just as damaging is emotional, psychological and spiritual abuse. God commands parents to use discipline and instruction approved by the Lord, when we raise children, "A*nd now a word to you fathers. Do not make your children angry; by the way, you treat them. Rather bring* *them up with the discipline and instruction approved by the Lord.* **Ephesians 6:4 NLT** Anything less is a form of abuse because the child enters adulthood without the proper tools to succeed in society.

I felt emotional and, psychological abuse a child. Like many victims of abuse, I failed to recognize how it affected me until later in life. I harbored an intense anger and self-hate that I turned on myself. I masked this with a nonchalant, careless attitude. I see this anger and self-hate in our young gang bangers. Instead of turning on themselves they kill, maim, and become desensitized to the violence. Usually, you can trace the root of their anti-social behavior to some form of abuse in their childhood.

When I looked into the eyes of the young men that stabbed me, I saw a hatred that made me shudder. I understood how at such a young age, they could hate to the point of murdering innocent victims. I felt the same anger, hurt and pain however; I took it out on myself instead of innocent victims. Many young people harbor the same hate and anger because someone gave up on them before they started living. It is a saying, "I do not care how much you know until I know how much you care." Some years back, I wrote a letter to the newspaper. I wrote:

"At the core, the Civil rights movement benefited those already poised to seize the opportunities that opened up. Sadly, a considerable segment of the African-American community remained behind. They perpetuate the vicious cycle of teen-age pregnancy, drugs, alcohol, crime and death by homicide or suicide.

Arguments abound about ideologies. Various groups point fingers at each other. Theories differ about the causes and solutions to these problems. One fact is certain; it is no longer just an inner-city problem. Like a cancer, these problems are spreading to every segment of American society.

Successful cancer treatment removes the cancer before it spreads. You remove cancer from the roots. It is ridiculous to think you can treat a cancer with a band-aid. It is just as ridiculous to build more jails, hire more police, come up with more pseudo-tough laws and penalties, and expect them to rid our cities and towns of crime.

Hopelessness lies at the root of many of these problems. People live in despair and believe no one cares about their plight in life. A person's environment profoundly affects their life. However, one can overcome their environment.

The message our inner-city children receive from cradle to grave is one of hopelessness. They receive it at home, school and through the media. They suffer rejection at the hands of a dominant racist society and class discrimination from middle-class African-Americans who refuse to look back and offer help.

I speak from experience. Seeds of rejection took root early in my young mind. These seeds grew into a tree of self-hatred bearing the fruits of a rage I did not understand. Instead of committing drive-by shootings, I turned my rage inward. Unconsciously, I attempted suicide via drugs and alcohol. Thankfully, someone who cared intervened and introduced me to Jesus Christ. Jesus did not have a hidden political agenda. He loved and accepted me with all of my flaws. This agape love produced a change on the inside of me that empowered me to change my circumstances.

More police and jails are band-aids unable to cure the cancer that threatens to destroy our country. Esoteric discussions about racism are useless unless followed by action. What we really need are people who care!"

Gang members find a sense of belonging and love however warped, in the gang Most of them missed that feeling at home. Unless they encounter someone, who genuinely cares enough about them to introduce them God, death or the penitentiary awaits them.

I head up the Prison Ministry at my church. I find that a great number of the incarcerated woman suffered some form of sexual abuse as a child. They cope by acting out and becoming promiscuous in later life. Other side effects of sexual abuse are unwanted pregnancy, guilt, shame, feelings of helplessness, low self-esteem, mistrust of others, prostitution, aggression, depression, emotional withdrawal, deficient social skills and the list goes on. Below I listed the most common types of abuse.

Types of Abuse

    a. **Physical abuse** – includes all acts that create injury or a substantial and unnecessary risk of injury. Recently, advocates against child abuse have criticized the Bible, claiming that it encourages child abuse. They take such scriptures as **(Proverbs 13:24)**, which says, *"If you refuse to discipline your children, it proves you don't love them; if you love your children, you will be prompt to discipline them"*, out of context. They say that this and other scriptures encourage physical abuse of children. The Bible does not exclude corporal punishment but clearly places all forms of child discipline in the context of love. Abuse stems from substance abuse, an abusive past, anger and poverty. Hurt people hurt people. Godly discipline leads to maturity; abuse produces dysfunction. [1]

    b. **Sexual abuse** – any form of sexual contact or conversation that exploits a child to bring sexual gratification to the exploiter. God abhors sexual abuse. Sexual abuse distorts a child's understanding of sex and its wholesome purpose within God's design. Sexual abuse interrupts a child's delicate process of emotional, social and sexual maturation. Sexual abuse confuses the progression (in a young mind from

accepting healthy human love to knowing the divine love of God. Sexual abuse is a transgression against the image of God and the temple of God. It is illicit sexual behavior directed against a child's very person. The abused child can find healing and the abuser can obtain forgiveness, but neither can happen without recognition of God's standards and commands. [2]
c. **Emotional and psychological abuse** – a pattern of blaming, belittling, verbally attacking, or rejecting a child, or demanding that a child assume responsibilities that he/she is incapable of handling. Some side effects of emotional and psychological abuse are guilt, mistrust of others, aggression, deficient social skills, emotional withdrawal and criminality. The bible teaches that children are our heritage and we should esteem them highly **(Psalm 127:3; Isaiah 49:15; Ephesians 6:4; Titus 2:4).** God warns against harming children in **(Luke 17:2).** God loves children, commands parents to love and nurture them, and will severely judge those who do them harm. [3]

Victims of abuse carry an enormous amount of bitterness and anger through life. Forgiveness is the key to victory over the deep-rooted bitterness and anger. It took many years for me to forgive and allow God to cleanse me of the anger and bitterness I carried inside. When I finally let it go, I enjoyed victory. If God forgave us, we can forgive others. He commands it in the Sermon on the Mount in the Lord's Prayer, He said, *"And forgive us our sins as we have forgiven those who have sinned against us (Matthew 6:12 NLT)."*

Discovery Questions

What type of abuse – if any – have you experienced as a child?

Have you forgiven the perpetrator of your abuse?

What secrets about any prior abuse cause you grief today?

Are you ready to forgive the perpetrator of this abuse?

Chapter 3

Shame on You

◈

Fear not: you will no longer live in shame. The shame of your youth and the sorrows of widowhood will be remembered no more (Isaiah 54: 4 NLT).

I gave my back to those who beat me and my cheeks to those who pull out my beard. I do not hide from shame, for they mock me and spit in my face (Isaiah 50:6 NLT).

I recall two incidents from my past that caused me great shame. The first occurred when I was about ten or eleven years old. While playing with my friends in the neighborhood, my father came home drunk, early from work. He urinated in front of all of us. My friends howled in laughter and teased me incessantly. I tried to play it off and laugh with them however; I felt shame for my father and did not know how to process the shame so I internalized it. The other incident occurred at my eighth grade graduation. My family could not afford a suit for me, so I wore an old shirt and tie. No one from my family showed up. After the graduation, while the other children enjoyed their families I walked alone to 79th street. I got drunk. I felt a mixture of anger, shame, self-pity and an intense loneliness. These and other experiences contributed to my shame-based personality. I did not feel good enough, strong enough or smart enough. I felt inadequate and unworthy even though I possessed a keen intellect and a sharp wit.

I sabotaged any success in my life because of an inherent sense of unworthiness. I accepted failure as something I deserved. I developed a loser's mentality and my life fulfilled the message that resided in my spirit. The voice always said, "You will not make it. Something will happen to mess up the happiness you are feeling." I looked for the other shoe to drop.

A sense of shame is one of the most toxic emotions we can experience. Modern medical understanding of addictions and compulsivity tells us that our drivenness is often an effort to escape from or compensate for a profound sense of shame and inadequacy. What is the shame that can envelop us and paralyze us? We may feel shame about our estrangement from God. We may harbor shame feelings about our inability to pull in the reins on addictive or compulsive behaviors. We may feel ashamed for the damage we have inflicted on others through our life-styles. We may carry shame about the dysfunction of our childhood families. [1]

King David knew about shame. He wrote, *"My dishonor is continually before me, and the shame of my face has covered me, because of the voice of him who reproaches and reviles, because of the enemy and the avenger (Psalm 44:15, 16 NKJV)."*

1. Shame defined

    a. We define shame as a deep-seated feeling that something is wrong with me. We feel inadequate and unworthy and develop a shame-based personality that keeps us from attaining the potential God intended for

our lives. Children from dysfunctional families can absorb shame directly or indirectly.
   i. Indirect shame can come from many sources:
      1. Parents' attitude can teach a child shame
      2. Children can feel shame for their parents' problems.
      3. Family secrets can produce shame.
      4. Abuse, in whatever form, can produce shame.
   ii. Direct shame comes from:
      1. Verbal abuse from family members i.e.
         a. "You're just like you're no good daddy."
         b. "You're stupid."
         c. "You ought to be ashamed of yourself."
      2. Peers transmit shame from cruel statements towards other children.
      3. Churches create shame by giving messages of condemnation instead of hope and grace. [2]
b. Shame originated in the Garden of Eden with Adam and Eve's sin **(Genesis 2:25; 3:10, 11)**.
c. A shame-based personality makes you want to hide who you really are. You wear a mask to avoid intimacy because of the fear that someone will see the real you.
d. Shame robs us of God's blessings because we do not feel worthy to receive them. It can mask itself as a sort of pseudo-humility. We live a life of defeat because we fail to exercise our faith in God.

2. The Process of Shame's Work

   e. You learn to feel shame as you grow up in a dysfunctional family.
   f. The shame develops into a shame-based personality.

g. The shame-based personality begins to have a drastic impact on how you think and act.
h. You engage in behavior that creates its own shame.
i. You deny the presence of shame in your life, through denial.[3]

3. **God's Remedy for Shame – Own It To Disown It**

   j. Talk about your shame with God through prayer **(Hebrews 4:15, 16)** realizing that Jesus bore our shame on the Cross of Calvary **(Isaiah 53:3-6)**.
   k. Share your shame, following the lead and guidance of the Holy Spirit, with a safe, trusted, spiritual Christian **(James 5:16; Galatians 6:1)**.
   l. Submit to the cleansing power of God **(Romans 8:1, 33-34; Isaiah 54:4; Psalm 25:3; Psalm 32:5; 1John 1:9)**.

m. Accept the cleansing of God, for guilt and shame. God said, *"Though your sins are like scarlet, I will make them white as snow. Though they are red like crimson, I will make them as white as wool (Isaiah 1:18 TLB)*. When we throw off the heavy weight of guilt and shame, it frees us to live an abundant life unencumbered by condemnation. The guilt and shame an addict feels never breaks the cycle; rather, it pushes him or her into another episode to escape how bad he feels. The answer is simple, and the answer is total forgiveness **(John 12:47)**.

Discovery Questions

Explain your understanding of shame.

What are some of the signs of a shame-based identity?

What are you ashamed of from your past?

How is shame holding you back from fulfilling God's purpose in your life?

What are your plans to rid yourself from shame? Be specific.

Explain the difference between shame and godly sorrow.

Chapter 4

The Many Faces of Addiction

When an evil spirit leaves a person, it goes into a desert, seeking rest but finding none. Then it says, "I will return to the person I came from." So it returns and finds its former home cleaned and empty, swept and clean. Then the spirit finds seven other spirits more evil than itself, and they all enter the person and live there. And so that person is worse off than before. That will be the experience of this evil generation (Matthew 12:43 – 45 NLT).

When God delivers us from any type of addiction, he expects us to fill the empty space caused by that addiction, with His Spirit **(Ephesians 3:19)**. The infilling of the Holy Spirit is an ongoing process. Just as the children of Israel received daily manna for their sustenance, we need a daily portion of God's Word and Spirit for our spiritual sustenance. Without it, we open the door for other addictions to enter our lives to take the place of our primary addiction. These addictions – which are spirits - see a clean house and they rush in to occupy it **(Matthew 12:43–45)**. I tried to fill my spiritual house with exercise, work, sex, prescription drugs, religion, and relationships but these unwanted tenants ruined my house. Our temples belong to God (**1Corinthians 6:19, 20**). We are God's property and His Spirit should be the only occupant in our spiritual houses.

Addictions come in all shapes, sizes and forms. Sin underlies all addiction and we all sin. We fall short of God's glory and allow denial to cheat us of our victory (**Romans 3:23; 1John 1:8-10**). Addictions are ultimately a disorder of worship. We usurp God's position as Lord of our lives and we replace Him with self. This is idolatry. Some addictive agents are:

- Alcohol or Drugs
- Work, achievement, and success
- Money addictions, such as overspending, gambling and hoarding
- Control addictions, especially if they surface in personal, sexual, family and business relationships
- Food addictions
- Sexual addictions
- Approval dependency (the need to please others)
- Rescuing patterns toward other persons
- Dependency on toxic relationships (relationships that are damaging or hurtful)
- Physical illness (hypochondria)
- Exercise and physical conditioning
- Cosmetics, clothes, cosmetic surgery, trying to look good on the outside
- Academic pursuits and excessive intellectualizing
- Religiosity or religious legalism (preoccupation with the forms and the rules and regulations of religion, rather than benefiting from the real spiritual message)
- General perfectionism

- Cleaning and avoiding contamination and other obsessive – compulsive symptoms
- Organizing, structuring (the need to always have everything in its place)
- Materialism [1]

This list can include anything. We owe God the throne of our hearts. Anything else is idolatry. He commanded us to place him first because He knew these other gods or addictions could not satisfy our needs **(Isaiah 44:6-20; Deuteronomy 6:5, 6; Mark 12:30, 31)**.

The AA Big Book describes addictions as cunning, baffling and powerful.[2] This sounds like how God described the serpent in the Garden of Eden **(Genesis 3:1)**. In the garden, the serpent lured Eve away from fellowship with God, by suggesting she could find happiness in disobedience. The serpent deceived her into thinking she could control her life and become as gods **(Genesis 3:4, 5)**.

Eve saw that the tree looked good, was good for food and would make her wise **(Genesis 3:6)**. Sin offers us the same empty promise only to plunge us into spiritual slavery and addiction **(Genesis 2:17; Romans 6:16)**. Satan uses the same tactics today. Addictions feel and look good and we think they will make us wise **(1John 2:16, 17)**. We try to satisfy our own spiritual, emotional and physical needs outside of Gods' will. We use some controllable external agent until we lose control and become slaves to our passions.

Our hearts deceive us into thinking we can find happiness apart from God **(Jeremiah 17:9)**. Triumph over addictions depends on our relationship with God. Through prayer, meditation and regular church attendance we develop godly habits that replace the negative ones. However, when God delivers us from a sin or addiction, a spiritual vacuum occurs. Unless the Holy Spirit and God's Word fill that vacuum, the enemy fills it with another addiction. This time the addiction might dress up and look respectable i.e. work and church however, the root problem of pride and selfishness remain. Secular recovery programs describe this as "stinking thinking." We might not practice our primary addiction, but we lug the same emotional luggage around with us. We must become compliant and allow God to break our self-will and pride before we can enjoy lasting victory.

Discovery Questions

Can you see yourself in the above list of addictions?

If so, what are you doing to seek help?

Describe a time in your life when you felt helpless about a behavior you were practicing.

How did you overcome the behavior?

Are you still tempted to act out with that behavior?

How do you handle the temptation?

Describe how religion or church can become an addiction.

What emotional baggage do you carry?

What hinders you from giving your emotional baggage to God?

Chapter 5

Who is in Control?

If you try to keep your life for yourself, you will lose it. But if you give up your life for me you will find true life (Luke 9:24 NLT).

He who has knowledge spares his words, and a man of understanding is of a calm (or cool) spirit Proverbs 17:27 NKJV).

*"I'm in control, never gonna stop.
Control, to get what I want
Control, I have to have a lot.
Control, now I am all grown up." Control – Janet Jackson 1986*

Janet's song topped the charts because of the strong dance rhythms and the catchy words. In addition, it topped the charts because most people desire control and could relate to the song.

The need to control is an insidious powerful compulsion that can wreck relationships and even lead to murder in extreme cases. Police can attest to the amount of restraining orders and domestic violence calls they receive because a person feels they are losing control in a relationship and resort to stalking and violence to regain it. The compulsion to control is characteristic of many people who experienced ongoing emotional pain during childhood.

When you grow up in a chaotic, dysfunctional environment, everything seems out of control. There is not any stability anywhere. The child learns not to trust anyone because of the onslaught of disappointments they faced growing up. Control then becomes a survival mechanism to deal with the turmoil. The philosophy of the child becomes, control feelings, control situations, control people because if you succeed at controlling, you will not get hurt. The problems arise when you realize you cannot control people, situations or in most cases feelings. Now what do you do? You become afraid of these feelings thinking they can and will destroy you. So you try to bury these feelings. They still live so they continue to sprout up and make you miserable. [2]

I see this need to control in teen-age mothers. They rebel against their parents and the world broadcasting, "You can't control me!" The baby becomes their ticket to adulthood and freedom. It will force their parents to accept them as adults and enable them to control their own lives. It will allow them to make decisions for themselves. More importantly, the baby gives them somebody that can reciprocate their love. Unfortunately, many of them lack parenting skills and the cycle of teen pregnancy continues from generation to generation.

Men with control issues develop the "pimp and player mentality." You hear rappers and street thugs constantly glorifying the lifestyle of the pimp. My friends and I grew up admiring the pimps in our neighborhood. These people exercised tremendous control over their prostitutes. We read Iceberg Slim's novel *"The Pimp"* and sought to emulate his tactics for controlling his women. We failed to read between the lines and recognize the pain and misery caused by such a lifestyle. Iceberg Slim whose real name is Robert Beck wrote in his novel *"The Naked Soul of Iceberg Slim"*, *"A scant few of the older career pimps I have known survive to old age. Drugs, whiskey, shootings stabbings and the debauchery of the fast life usually doom them to a coffin in early middle age."* [3]

We knew this yet the intoxicating allure of control still doomed many young men and women to early deaths. Beck said in another place, *"What makes young guys itch to pimp is the popular belief that a pimp's life is dream stuff, like gangs of sexy girls and money and night-clubbing. But trauma for trauma the pimp's life is perhaps the worst type of life anybody could live. He is feared, hated, despised and walks a greased wire with the penitentiary on one side and his death on the other."* [4] Sadly, this deadly trap still entangles our young people today. I recently saw a young man that did not fit the stereotypical mold of inner-city dysfunction wearing a green T-shirt that read, "Pimps wear green shirts." This shows how far reaching this mentality has grown.

Control issues wreck relationships. These issues restrict the ability to express true feelings. The streets encourage one to hide true emotions as a survival tactic. Life or death sometimes depended on how well you controlled your emotions. Robert Beck learned early in his pimping career to hide his emotions, hence the nickname Iceberg Slim. I learned to bury my true feelings growing up in a dysfunctional family and this bled into my relationships as an adult. I think this contributed to my two divorces. It took years for me to describe my true feelings and even today, I struggle with this issue. This tendency to bury my feelings affected my prayer life. God desires truthful worship **(John 4:24)** and I struggled with honesty. Honesty is the foundation for any relationship especially our relationship with God.

In women, control issues hinder submission to their husbands in a marriage. Paul wrote in his Epistle to the Ephesians, *"You wives will submit to your husbands as you do to the Lord. For a husband is the head of his wife as Christ is the head of his body, the church; he gave his life to be her Savior. As the church submits to Christ, so you wives submit to your husbands* in *everything (Ephesians 5:22–24 NLT).* Submission requires a trust that some women lack because of a dysfunctional past. Because of this control issue, the fabric of the marriage weakens and unless both partners submit to God's Word, it will fail.

In the same Ephesians passage of scripture, Paul tells men to love their wives as Christ loved the church. He said, *"And you husbands must love your wives with the same love Christ showed the church. He gave up his life for her (Ephesians5:25).* This type of supportive love makes it easier for a woman to learn submissiveness in a relationship. It builds trust and a sense of security in the woman. Men must leave the pimp and player mentality in the streets and develop a Christ mentality for a successful marriage.

Control issues in church create disorder. God placed spiritual heads over us and when we chose to disobey or not listen to them, we invite spiritual trouble into our lives. *"Obey your spiritual leaders and do what they say. Their work is to watch over your souls, and they know they are accountable to god. Give them reason to do this joyfully and not with sorrow. That would certainly not be for your benefit (Hebrews 13:17 NLT).* Our desire to control will lead us into disobedience and the ministry God entrusted to our care will suffer because we fail to listen to spiritual guidance **(Proverbs 4: 20–23).** This craving for control causes church splits and stirs animosity among members. People jockey for positions in the church to gain power and control. Many tenderhearted young saints leave because they see the ugliness of the power struggles among the leaders.

The compulsion to control is repulsive and satanic in nature. It along with pride is at the root of every addiction. I turned to alcohol and drugs because they gave me a predictable feeling and a semblance of control. I could pick my feeling according to the substance I bought to alter my moods. Anything or anybody I felt I could not control I wrote off as insignificant.

I practiced denial and labeled it "cool." It was my feeble attempt to maintain some control. Growing up on the streets of Chicago, we mimicked the older "cool cats" that hung out on the corner. As I grew older and started getting high with these "cool cats", I saw through their false pose of cool. Like me, they put on a cool façade to cover their pain and insecurity.

Bell Hooks, in her book, *"We Real Cool, Black Men and Masculinity"* defines cool. She said, *"Once upon a time black male cool was defined by the ways in which black men confronted the hardships of life without allowing their spirits to become ravaged. They took the pain of it and used it alchemically to turn the pain into gold. That burning process required high heat. Black male cool was defined by the ability to withstand the heat and remain centered. It was defined by black male willingness to confront reality, to face the truth, and bear it not by adopting a false pose of cool while feeding on fantasy; not by black male denial or by assuming a "poor me" victim identity. It was defined by individual black males daring to self-define rather than be defined by others."* [5] Illinois Senator Barack Obama, reflects this type of coolness. Coolness is control under pressure.

Salvation taught me the meaning of coolness. It means letting go of our anxieties and giving God control of our lives. It is ironic that in God's Kingdom, to gain control you must lose control.

Paul said in his Epistle to the Philippians, *"Don't worry about anything; instead pray about everything. Tell God what you need, and thank him for all that He has done. If you do this, you will experience God's peace, which is far more wonderful than the human mind can understand. His peace will guard your hearts and minds as you live in Christ Jesus (Philippians 4:6, 7)."* These scriptures capture the fundamental nature of cool. Paul wrote this from a dungeon, imprisoned for preaching the Gospel. Cool and calm, he faced this adversity and encouraged others in the process. Paul's trust in God formed his coolness. Surrender to God makes you cool.

Trust in God gives us freedom from the compulsion to control. Our past disappointments make it hard to trust anyone. Relationship builds trust. The more we strengthen our relationship with God, the easier it becomes to trust Him. The wise King Solomon wrote in Proverbs, *"Trust in the Lord with all your heart; do not depend on your own understanding. Seek his will in all you do and he will direct your paths (Proverbs 3:5, 6).*

The Life Recovery Bible says, *"It is not uncommon to link our perception about God to our childhood experiences with people who played powerful roles in our life. If people who were capricious, abusive, distant, uncaring, or incompetent have victimized us in the past, we may now anticipate these qualities in God. We may have learned in the past that putting confidence in people only brings disappointment. We cannot let this keep us from ever trusting again."* [6]

The Bible tells us that, *"God is not a man that He should lie. He is not a human, that he should change His mind (Numbers 23:19 NLT)."* He said, *"I will never fail you. I will never forsake you (Hebrews 13:5 NLT)."*

Dr. Henry Cloud, in his book, *"The Secret Things of God"* states, "Opening yourself up to the gifts of God means trusting that he loves you and will provide for you. It means daring to be vulnerable with both God and the right people. It often means trusting beyond what you can see. It means believing in the character of God even more than you believe in your desired outcome. God's blessing awaits you. You hold the key that unlocks them: trust." [7]

I laugh to myself when people comment about my "old school coolness." I say to myself, if they only knew. If you want, real control and real cool learn to trust God! This is positive control. This is self-control, which is a fruit of the Holy Spirit **(Galatians 5:22, 23; 2Peter 1:6)**. The Life Recovery Bible says, *"Self-control is not willpower. It is not something we get by gritting our teeth and forcing ourselves to "just say no." God calls self-control a fruit. Fruit does not instantly pop out on the tree. As the tree grows and the seasons pass, the fruit naturally develops. As we continue to follow God's guidance, taking one step at a time, our self-control will gradually grow. Our job is to stay connected to God. It is the Holy Spirit's job to produce the fruit of self-control in our life. Self-control is something that comes, as we grow closer to God. As we take one step at a time, one day at a time, God will give us his own character."*[8]

Through self-control, the Holy Spirit teaches us to delay gratification. We learn to wait on God. Esau lost his birthright because he could not delay gratification. He had to satisfy his hunger on the spot and sold his birthright to Jacob for a bowl of stew **(Genesis 25: 27 – 34)**. We often miss God's best for our lives because we have not learned to wait. We settle for good and miss great. We search for shortcuts to happiness and faster and easier ways to satisfy our needs. We want instant deliverance from our problems.

God takes us the long way to teach us patience and instill in us the ability to delay gratification. It took the children of Israel forty years to accomplish an eleven-day trip **(Deuteronomy 1:2, 3)**. God does not believe in shortcuts or quick fixes. He prolonged the Israelite's journey to teach them trust. He taught them how to enjoy freedom and how to wage spiritual warfare. Paul said, *"All these events* *happened to them as examples for us. They were written down to warn us, who live at the time when this age is drawing near (1Corinthians 10:11 NLT).* We should learn from their experience. Our wilderness experiences build the character of Christ in us **(Romans 8:29).** Jesus modeled this for us when he refused Satan's offer to give him the kingdoms of the world **(Matthew 4:8 -10).** Instead, he chose God's way and died on the cross for our sins. He gained the kingdoms of the world the right way.

King David learned this principle and wrote, *"Be still in the presence of the Lord and wait patiently for him to act. Do not worry about evil people who prosper or fret about their evil schemes (Psalm 37:7)."*

Discovery Questions

What type of trust issues are you dealing with, in your relationships, job, church, etc.?

What can you do to improve your personal relationship with God? Be specific.

When will you start implementing your plan?

What are some situations in which you feel a strong need to control?

Describe a situation where you felt out of control. How did you handle it?

Chapter 6

The Past Is Past

Keep on asking, and you will be given what you ask for. Keep on looking, and you will find. Keep on knocking, and the door will be opened. For everyone who asks, receives. Everyone who seeks finds. And the door is opened to everyone who knocks (Matthew 7:7, 8 NLT).

Jesus gave us the solution for victory over our past in the Gospel of Matthew **(Matthew 7: 7, 8)**. For simplicity let us use the acronym for ask. In these scriptures, Jesus said **A**sk, **S**eek and **K**nock.

A	Ask Jesus Christ to save you and transform your mind (Romans 10:9, 10; 12:2). Acknowledge your problem, "own it to disown it" (John 8:32, 36; John 16:13). Accept and obey God's plan for deliverance (Proverbs 3:5, 6; 1Samuel 15:22, 23).
S	Seek God's Kingdom before you seek worldly counsel (Matthew 6:33). Submit to God's authority (James 4:7). Strengthen yourself with God's power (Ephesians 3:16; 6:10). Set your mind on godly thoughts (2Corinthians 10:3-5; Philippians 4:8). Share your testimony and serve others (Galatians 5:13; Luke 8:39).

K	**Knock** on God's doors until you receive an answer, persist in prayer (1Thessalonians 5:17; Luke 18:1-8). **Keep** yourself studying and meditating on the Word (Psalm 1:1-3; Joshua 1:8; 2Timothy 2:15). **Know** and believe that every Word of God is true (1Peter 1:23-25; Isaiah 40:8; John 17:17; 2Peter 1:20, 21) and faith in God's Word can deliver us from the pain of our past.

Ask Jesus Christ to save you and change your heart **(Romans 10:9, 10)**. This is the first step of deliverance. Cooperate with the Holy Spirit as he supervises the process of Sanctification in your life. Sanctification removes dysfunction and enables us to function as God intended. We could not control our family of origin or the abuse we suffered as children however; we can control our responses to them. Ask God for the grace to forgive anyone who has hurt us and to remove any bitterness lodged in our hearts **(Hebrews 12:15; Matthew 6:12-15)**. God sent Jesus to die for our sins and this includes our dysfunction and our past.

The first step to any lasting deliverance is to allow Jesus Christ to have Lordship over our lives. This includes admitting our powerlessness to help ourselves. It is a lifelong process but God will finish the work **(Philippians 1:6; 2:13)**. This principle includes developing a close relationship with God and feeling comfortable enough to ask Him to meet our needs. James wrote, in his Epistle; *and yet the reason you* *do not have what you want is that you do not ask God for it (James 4:2b NLT).*

S – **Seek** daily and submit to the sanctifying power of the Holy Spirit **(James 4:7)**. Allow the Holy Spirit to search our spirits and uncover the root causes of our dysfunction **(Lamentations 3:40; Psalm 19:12; Psalm 139:23, 24)**. Once uncovered, give them to God **(1Peter 5:7)** – "own them to disown them." Seek God for guidance before you make any decision **(Proverbs 3:5, 6)**. Seek God for daily wisdom to handle the dilemmas we encounter in life. God said through Jeremiah, *"In those days when you pray, I will listen. If you look for me in earnest, you will find me when you seek me. I will be found by you, "says the Lord. I will end your captivity and restore your fortunes. I will gather you at of the nations where I sent you and bring you home again to your own land (Jeremiah 29:12 – 14 NLT)."*

K – **Knock** on Heavens doors. God invites us to come before His throne to obtain mercy and grace to live our daily lives **(Hebrews 4:16)**. This means, if you fall get back up **(1John 1:9)**. God wiped all condemnation from our slates when we accepted Jesus Christ as our Savior **(Romans 8:1)**. Keep yourself in the Word because the Word cleanses our emotions and transforms our minds **(Psalm 119:9; Romans 12:1)**. Finally, keep your spiritual armor on because the spiritual war for your mind and heart never ceases **(Ephesians 6:10-18; 1Peter 4:7)**. Knocking takes persistence and patience. Like the widow in the Gospel of Luke, do not cease praying, your change is coming **(Luke 18:1 – 8)**.

Part 3

Biblical Applications for the Twelve Steps

The steps of the godly are directed by the Lord. He delights in every detail of their lives. Though they stumble they will not fall, for the Lord holds them in his hand (Psalm 37:23, 24 NLT).

Chapter 1

History of the 12 Step Programs

Dr. Frank Buchman had a spiritual awakening in 1908 (he was saved). He helped form the Oxford Group, which operated from the spiritual principles of surrender, restitution and sharing. This came from an earlier move of the Holy Spirit called the Oxford movement in the early 1800's. Members of this group conducted house meetings, which included testimonies, personal witness, Bible study and personal talks. Members were encouraged to find and work with persons suffering from problems similar to theirs.

In 1934, Bill Wilson, the founder of Alcoholics Anonymous, traced his sobriety to the witness of one his friends Ebby Thatcher. Thatcher was involved with the Oxford Group and shared Jesus with Bill. Bill experienced the supernatural touch of God as he underwent treatment in the hospital for acute alcoholism. A year later, he felt a strong urge to drink. He knew that he could only retain his sobriety if he reached out to others suffering as he did. He linked up with Dr. Bob Smith, an alcoholic surgeon. Finally, after days of witnessing Dr. Bob accepted Christ and stopped drinking. Together, in 1937, they formed Alcoholics Anonymous and wrote the **12 Steps,** borrowing from the spiritual principles Bill Wilson learned at the Oxford Group.

The general principles underlying the recovery process are:

1. admission of an overpowering problem, such as alcoholism, drug addiction or compulsive gambling;
2. reliance on a power greater than oneself, for example, whatever concept of God the member may hold;
3. self-examination – that is, taking "a searching and fearless moral inventory" of oneself;
4. confidential disclosure to a more experienced group member of wrongs done;
5. restitution;
6. service to others who suffer from the same problem. [1]

Today, we have 12 Step programs for every type of addiction. During the course of my life, I attended many secular 12 Step meetings, only to leave empty. I heard group leaders teach such foolishness about higher powers. They promoted idolatry by saying anything can serve as your higher power – even a chair. I felt like Paul when he confronted the Greeks about their unknown god **(Acts 17:23)**.

God inspired me to write this 12 Step Program with Christian Applications to correlate the truths of Gods Word with the concepts of the 12 Step program. I understand that any program without God is empty. Any recovery plan without Jesus Christ as its center is empty. David said in **(Psalm 37:23 NLT)** – *The steps of the godly are directed by the Lord. He delights in every detail of their lives.* A robust recovery demands that we become doers of the Word, instead of just hearers **(James 1:22-25)**. First, we need to know the One and True God and experience salvation through His Son, Jesus Christ **(John 14:6)**.

In addition, when we engage in an active relapse prevention program we reduce the chances of falling back into our old habits. Recovery from addiction is like walking up a down escalator. It is impossible to stand still. When you stop moving forward, you find yourself moving backwards. You do not have to do anything in particular to develop symptoms that lead to relapse. The symptoms develop spontaneously in the absence of a strong recovery program. Relapse does not simply mean returning to the acting-out behavior. Those in relapse will begin to exhibit the behavior patterns and attitudes they practiced when they were dysfunctional. Recovery circles call this "stinking thinking."

The Twelve Steps with Christian Applications provide a structured and biblical way of dealing with our addictions. Peter admonishes us to, *"Be careful! Watch out for attacks from the devil, your great enemy. He prowls around like a roaring lion, looking for some victim to devour (1Peter 5:8 TLB)*. Other versions of the Bible translate careful as sober. Unless we engage God in a strong personal relationship we can end up on our backs looking up, wondering what happened. *If you think you are standing strong, be careful, for you, too, may fall into the same sin. But remember that the temptations that come into your life are no different from what others experience. And* **God is faithful.** *He will keep the temptation from becoming so strong that you cannot stand against it. When you are tempted, He will show you a way out so that you will not give in to it (1Corinthians 10:12, 13)*

After salvation, God develops us through sanctification. God uses our life experiences to mold us in the image of Christ and to mature us in his Word. We grow when we cooperate with the Holy Spirit and respond to our trials and tribulations in a godly way **(James 1:2-4)**. We chose our responses. Peter outlines this process in his second epistle, he said, *"So make every effort to apply the benefits of these promises to your life. Then your faith will produce a life of moral excellence. A life of moral excellence leads to knowing God better. Knowing God leads to self-control. Self-control* *leads to patient endurance, and patient endurance leads to godliness. Godliness leads to love for other Christians and finally you will grow to have genuine love for everyone. The more you grow like this, the more you will become productive and useful in your knowledge of our Lord Jesus Christ (2Peter 1:5-8 NLT)."* Every trial presents opportunities for us to respond with a godly response. Obedience to this process prevents relapse: *"So, dear brothers and sisters, work hard to prove that you really are among those God has called and chose. Doing this you will never stumble or fall away (2Peter 1:10 NLT)."*

Tim Sledge in his book "Moving Beyond Your Past," talks about the Cycles of Recovery and the Cycles of Pain. We all begin at the same place with emotional pain. We chose what cycle we want to jump on. The cycle of pain begins with denial that leads to blaming which results in shame. We then become self-sufficient and start striving that brings exhaustion (sick and tired of being sick and tired). Finally, we become bulletproof and avoid our problems that drive us to loneliness. The dominating attitudes that fuel these behaviors are denial and control. We go through the cycle of pain repeatedly, digging grooves of bondage into our minds until we decide to move up to the cycle of recovery.

In the cycle of recovery, we start at the same place as with the cycle of pain – emotional pain. However, we chose godly responses and our emotional pain leads to victory. We start this cycle with honesty about our condition, which leads to confession and cleansing. This develops an openness that positions us to ask God to supply our needs. This brings empowering, which allows us to become vulnerable enough to share our experiences. This promotes intimacy with God and people. An attitude of brokenness and surrender stimulate the cycle of recovery. [2]These attitudes hold up the foundations of any successful recovery program or victorious

Christian walk. I included these spiritual principles in the first nine of the twelve steps with Christian applications. I taught these principles for two years at the B.A.I.T Ministry Christian Center lead by Pastor Bernice Garner. I saw God deliver entire families of entrenched strongholds that hid behind religion and tradition. We uncovered layers of denial and shame and faced some issues that chained us to lives of defeat and mediocrity. It takes hard work and a willingness to cooperate with the Holy Spirit but I know if we apply the same rigor to God's plan as we did to our addictions, victory is ours!

Chapter 2

Biblical Applications For The Twelve steps

1. We admitted we were powerless over _____ and that our life has become unmanageable.

Biblical Application:

Anything or anybody we depend on to meet our spiritual, emotional and physical needs besides God becomes an idol in our life. This is a sin. The list can include drugs, alcohol, gambling, sex, money, food, relationships, exercise, church work, hypochondria, and materialism. This list is not exhaustive and includes anything external we use to meet an internal need. As a result, our lives become unmanageable. In Step One, we face our denial and admit our powerlessness over these dependencies.

Related Scriptures:
Psalm 51; 1Corinthians 10: 14; 2Corinthians 10: 3-6; Romans 7: 18-20

Spiritual Principle – Brokenness

2. We came to believe that <u>faith in our Lord and Savior Jesus Christ</u> could restore us to sanity.

Biblical Application:

We realize we cannot change ourselves. Our dependencies have become too powerful for us to handle and our attempts to control our addiction has failed. Step Two, is an outgrowth of Step 1. In Step One, we admitted our own powerlessness, so logically we seek a new source of strength to take charge for us. That strength is a saving faith in Jesus Christ, who can restore us to sanity (wellness and wholeness).

Related Scriptures:
2Corinthians 5: 17; Luke 15: 11-32; Philippians 2: 13

Spiritual Principle – Brokenness

3. Made a decision to turn our will and life over to the <u>care of God through faith in His Son Jesus Christ</u>.

Biblical Application:

We decide to give God <u>complete</u> control of our lives. We accept Jesus Christ as our personal Savior and repent (turn away) from our sin and turn to God for help. We allow the Holy Spirit to empower us for living a life that is free from bondage. Addictions and excessive compulsions are counterfeit means of trying to meet our most basic physical, emotional and spiritual hungers. With God's help, we can find genuine ways of satisfying these needs.

Related Scriptures:
Romans 10: 8-13; Romans 6: 16; Ephesians 2: 8-10

Spiritual Principal – Surrender

4. We made a searching and fearless moral inventory of ourselves.

Biblical Application:

In this step, we allow the Holy Spirit to aid us in discovering the <u>root</u> of our addictions and compulsions. In most cases, this means we have to examine our childhood. What negative message or experience from our past is keeping us in bondage? Are there any lingering resentment, fear, insecurity and shame that we have not given to God? Are we carrying the heavy burden of guilt for the pain we have inflicted on others and ourselves because of our dependencies? In this personal inventory, we allow the Word of God to expose anything that is hindering us in our walk with Him. This takes courage! Also as a counterbalancing agent, we should acknowledge and list our positive attributes. It helps to write these on paper.

Related Scriptures:
Psalm139: 23, 24, Lamentation 3: 40

Spiritual Principle – Honesty

5. We admitted to God, to ourselves, and to another human being the exact nature of our wrongs.

Biblical Application:

Our secrets or skeletons that we carry because of our dependencies oftentimes force us to live a life of isolation. We go through life wearing the mask of denial. No one knows and we are unable to share the <u>real</u> person who lives inside of us. In this step we come clean with God (who already knows us), ourselves and at least one other person about the pain and suffering we have endured because of our addiction. We can share what we have found out about ourselves in Step 4. As we do this, we experience a spiritual, emotional and sometimes physical healing. We now can help someone experiencing similar problems as our own.

Related Scriptures:
James 5: 16; 1John 1: 8-10; Genesis 3: 9-11

Spiritual Principal – Confession

6. We were entirely ready to have God remove all these defects of character.

Biblical Application:

After we have conducted a thorough and fearless moral inventory, we uncover many sins in our life that need cleansing. These sins can become secondary addictions and dependencies. These and all addictions are cunning, baffling and powerful. We still enjoy and want to cling to them however; they are as dangerous as our primary addiction. If we are not careful, we will substitute one addiction for another. God's will is to sanctify us. He desires to develop in us a heart that is willing to give up <u>everything</u> that is contrary to Him.

Related Scriptures:
John 5: 1-15; Romans 6: 11-14; Psalm 19: 12, 13; Mark 9: 14-29

Spiritual Principle – Openness

7. Humbly asked God to remove our defects of character.

Biblical Application:

Both Steps Six and Seven emphasize the importance of God's intervention in addressing our character defects. Step Six focused on our <u>willingness</u> to yield our character defects to God. In Step 7, we <u>humbly</u> ask God to intervene and remove our defects of character. Sadly, most of the time we must" hit bottom" before we decide to look up and realize the Love of God. Hitting bottom is simply the negative results we reap because of sowing foolishness into our lives. God allows these consequences to humble us and bring us to our knees in prayer. Then and only then, can He mold us into the image of His Son Jesus Christ.

Related Scriptures:
James 4: 6-10; 2Chronicles 7:14; Philippians 2: 5-9

Spiritual Principle – Asking

8. Made a list of all the people we had harmed, and became willing to make amends to them all.

Biblical Application:

We harm many people in our lives, beside ourselves, because of our addiction. The list includes our children, spouses, and parents, work families, church families, community families, extended families and the family of man (other political, religious and racial groups). In our selfish pursuit to satisfy our addiction, we bulldoze our way through life, disregarding the hurt feelings and the broken relationships we have caused along the way. In Step 8, we ask the Holy Spirit to reveal the people we have harmed and give us the courage to ask amends. This list also includes those we feel have injured us. It is our responsibility to release them from the stronghold of unforgiveness. Lastly, self-forgiveness is necessary for total deliverance.

Related Scriptures:

Matthew 18: 21-35, Luke 6: 27-38, Luke 19: 8, Matthew 7: 1-5, Matthew 6: 14, 15

Spiritual Principal – Vulnerability

9. We made direct amends to such persons wherever possible, except when to do so would injure them or others.

Biblical Application:

This step is a continuation of Step 8. In Step 8, we were <u>willing</u> to make amends and in Step 9, we take action.
Amends include:

   a.) Sincere efforts to offer apology for past harm.
   b.) Wonderful bridge-builders for more positive future relationships.
   c.) Effective agents for removing the tremendous weight of guilt, shame and remorse.

We ask God for His direction and His wisdom to carry out this step correctly. The Holy Spirit will guide us to the people we need to make amends with and give us the correct words to say. Correct timing is important because when we make amends sometimes we open fresh wounds and ill feelings resurface. We have to let the healing process complete itself. Finally, the people we extend amends to may not reciprocate by forgiving us. Still, there is freedom and healing in making amends.

Related Scriptures:
Matthew 5: 23,24; Luke 19: 8; Isaiah 50: 4,5; Proverbs 16: 7; James 1: 5

Spiritual Principle – Sharing

10. We continued to take personal inventory, and when we were wrong, promptly admitted it.

Biblical Application:

Steps 10, Eleven and Twelve are maintenance steps. Daily prayer and meditation are extremely important parts of our Christian walk. We cannot afford to allow the cares of the world rob us of our communion with God. Daily diligence is necessary to maintain our freedom in God. Our enemy Satan is lurking in the shadows waiting to pounce on us. He wants to destroy our testimony, steal our joy and eventually kill us. He cannot pluck us from God's hand however; he can make us ineffective for Kingdom work. If you fall, immediately get back up! Ask God for forgiveness, then accept His forgiveness and keep stepping. Stand in the power God has given us.

Related Scriptures:
Mark 14: 38; 1Corinthians 10: 12; Matthew 12: 43-45; Luke 11: 24-26; 2Peter 1:3-8; Galatians 5: 22, 23

Spiritual Principle – Perseverance

11. Sought through prayer and meditation to improve our conscious contact with God, praying for the knowledge of His will and the power to carry it out.

Biblical Application:

Step 11 builds on Step Ten. Prayer, meditation and church attendance are vital tools for lasting spiritual growth. Christian literature and Christian music help keep our mind in a consecrated state. Review your list of your positive personality qualities that you listed in Step 5. Then use them to bless the Body of Christ (your local church). Ask the Holy Spirit to guide you to the ministry God has ordained for your life. Finally determine in your heart to grow in grace and in the knowledge of our Lord and Savior Jesus Christ.

Related Scriptures:
Philippians 4: 6-9; Psalm 1:1-3; Joshua 1:6-9; Colossians 1:9,10; Ephesians 3: 14-19; Ephesians 1: 14-19; Matthew 6:10; Matthew 26: 39; Jeremiah 29: 11-12; Matthew 6:33

Spiritual Principle – Godliness

12. Having had a spiritual awakening as the result of our faith in Jesus Christ, we carried His message to others, and we practiced His Word in all of our affairs.

Biblical Application:

God delivered us from our addictions and dependencies so we can carry the message of reconciliation to a dying world. As we practice God's Word in our lives, we become a light to those around us still living in darkness. The ideal person to relate to someone bound by an addiction is someone delivered from that same addiction. We can talk the talk; however, we must walk the walk. As we practice these steps, empowered by the Holy Ghost, people will take notice and ask the question "what must I do to be saved?"

We have to tell somebody! The more we share our testimonies of deliverance the more empowered we become.

Related Scriptures:
1Timothy 1: 12-16; 2Corinthians 5: 19-20; Mark 16:14-18; Matthew 28:18-20; Mark 5: 1-20

Spiritual Principle – Charity

Definitions

Addiction – *Bondage to the rule of a substance, activity or state of mind, which then becomes the center of life, defending itself from the truth so that even bad consequences do not bring repentance, and leading to further estrangement from God.*

Addiction Cycle – *Pain > Reaching out for addictive agent > Temporary relief > Negative consequences > More pain.*

Hitting Bottom – *Negative results, we reap because of sowing foolishness and sin in our lives. It is a painful encounter with the consequences of our addictions. This bottom can be physical, emotional or spiritual.*

Denial – *All the false beliefs and excuses that hide our addictions.*

Stronghold - *Any thing that exalts itself in our minds, pretending to be bigger or more powerful than God **(2Corinthians 10: 3-5)**. It steals our focus and causes us to feel controlled, overpowered and mastered.*

Idol – *Anything or anybody we depend on to supply our needs besides God.*

Sanity – *Soundness of judgment.*

Insanity – *Doing the same things, expecting different results.*

- **Isolation** – *Sense of aloneness we feel when we try to hide our addictions. Our sins separate us from God **(Isaiah 59: 2)**. This causes us to feel lonely and isolated until we confess them.*
- **Amends** – *Repairing the damage of the past, to make better by some change, improve ones conduct.*
- **Inventory** – *Complete list of goods.*
- **Humility** – *We see ourselves as God sees us.*
- **Prayer** – *Dialogue between God and His people, especially His covenant partners.*
- **Meditation** – *Concentration on spiritual things and God's Word as a form of private devotion.*
- **Ambassador** – *An authorized representative or messenger (2Corinthians 5: 19-20).*
- **Commission** – *The authority to act for, in behalf of, or in place of another.*

Discovery Questions

What are you doing to maintain your freedom from addictions?

Is church attendance enough to keep us free from the bondage of addictions? Explain why or why not.

In your own words, define freedom.

How does freedom feel and what does it look like?

I recently visited my hometown, Chicago.
As usual, like a kid at recess, the anticipation of visiting my old neighborhood filled me with excitement.
I drove down Interstate 55, playing my oldies but goodies,
as my memory banks flooded with sweet thoughts of the "back in the day".
I drove to the hood and stared at faces, hoping to recognize beneath the ravages of time and just living, an old school mate or girlfriend or anybody that could connect me with the "back in the day".
I did not see anyone. Everybody was gone or had moved away.
I passed an old joint called "Another Place", and it was boarded up.
An intense sadness covered me like a dark cloud before a thunderstorm.
Because, you see, Another Place, to me, represented success, achievement, and exclusiveness.
Only the politically connected, the bourgeoisie or wannabe bourgeoisie (you know what) hung out there.

They had a rule, which excluded the neighborhood thugs, so that left me out.

I never saw the inside of Another Place.

Then, I realized that God has taken me to "Another Place".

He took the boarded up, run down, rat-infested places of my life and He built me a new building.

He took my building with the condemned sign on it and replaced it with a sign that says, "No more condemnation".

He tore down my projects and built me up as a spiritual temple.

However, to get to Another Place I had to let go of the other place that kept me tied to Egypt and spiritual slavery.

Because the "good old days" was not so good and right now beats "back in the day."

My sadness lifted when I understood that finally, I am in Another Place.

"Another Place" – author Alfred Long

Conclusion

Recently I sat at I Hop, and enjoyed a breakfast of steak, eggs and pancakes. When the server gave me my check, I proudly asked her to subtract my senior citizen discount from the total. To redeem a senior citizen discount represented a huge milestone for me.

I reminisced about the conversations – about longevity - I had in my youth. My friends and I lived with the shadow of death dogging our steps and we often voiced that we would die before the age of thirty. A rush of emotions filled my mind as I reflected on the memory of my friends that died before they could really enjoy life. The false glamour and allure of drugs, alcohol and the streets set them up for murder. John said in his Gospel, *"The thief's purpose is to steal and kill and destroy. My purpose is to give life in all of its fullness (John 10:10 NLT)*. The thief stole their youth, destroyed their lives and eventually killed them.

A wave of gratitude filled my heart as I thought of the grace and mercy of God, in my life. Rightfully, I deserved death, because I lived the same lifestyle as my friends but God had other plans. God said through Jeremiah, *"For I know the plans I have for you," says the Lord." They are plans for good and not for disaster, to give you a future and a hope (Jeremiah 29:11 NLT).*

Marvin Sapp sang, *"Lord, I never would have made it, I never could have made it without you. I would have lost my mind without you. Now I see how you were there for me and I am here today. I'm stronger, I'm wiser and I'm better."*

All that happened in my life, happened for my good **(Romans 8:28)** I am stronger, better and wiser! Amen!

Endnotes

Part 1

Chapter 1
1. Quincy Jones, *The Autobiography of Quincy Jones* (Doubleday, 2001), 19, 20.
2. Paul "The Waiter" Ricca, (Wikipedia)
3. Dr. Henry Cloud, *The Secret Things Of God* (Howard, 2007), 151.

Chapter 5
1. William Glasser, M.D., *Positive Addiction* (Harper & Row, 1976), 52.

Part 2

Chapter 1

1. Edward T. Welch, *Addictions A Banquet In The Grave* (P&R, 2001), preface.
2. Tim Sledge, *Making Peace With Your Past* (Lifeway, 1992), 141–143.
3. Ibid., 10-17.

Chapter 2
1. Josh Mc Dowell, *Handbook On Counseling Youth* (W, 1996), 359.
2. Ibid., 347, 352.
3. Ibid., 347, 362

Chapter 3
1. Robert Hemfelt; Richard Fowler, *Serenity A Companion for Twelve Step Recovery* (Thomas Nelson, 1990), 19.
2. Tim Sledge, *Making Peace With Your Past* (Lifeway, 1992), 46, 47.
3. Ibid., 46-54.

Chapter 4
1. Robert Hemfelt; Richard Fowler, *Serenity Companion For Twelve Step Recovery* (Thomas Nelson, 1990), 13, 14.
2. Alcoholic's Anonymous (Alcoholic Anonymous World Services, Inc, 1995).

Chapter 5
1. Janet Jackson, (Lyrics, Google.com)
2. Tim Sledge, *Making Peace With Your Past* (Lifeway, 1992), 34.
3. Iceberg Slim, *The Naked Soul of Iceberg Slim* (Holloway House, 1971), 69.
4. Ibid., 60.
5. Bell Hooks, *We Real Cool, Black Men and Masculinity* (Routledge, 2004), 147.
6. The Life Recovery Bible, (Tyndale House Publishers, Inc., 1998).
7. Dr. Henry Cloud, *The Secret Things Of God* (Howard, 2007), 28.

8. The Life Recovery Bible, (Tyndale House Publishers, Inc., 1998), 1413.

Part 3

Chapter 1
1. Robert Hemfelt; Richard Fowler, *Serenity A Companion for Twelve Step Recovery* (Thomas Nelson, 1990), 19.
2. Tim Sledge, *Moving Beyond Your Past* (Lifeway, 1993).

Printed in the United States
204163BV00001B/343-471/P